"He used to have that 'I hate you' kind of thing and lately he's been running up and hugging me, no problem."

—Peter R, father of a five-year-old

"He used to have major tantrums, hitting himself, throwing himself against the wall. Now we might have a minor tantrum now and then, but then he calms down."

—Dan S, father of a six-year-old

"I remember starting the program and thinking, if I could only feel there is some hope here, I'd be so happy by this time next year. I never dreamed he'd emerge so tuned in, so vocal, so inquisitive, so loving, so aware and so happy. I'll never stop singing the praises of qigong. I hope that this method becomes much more common for helping autistic children. You've literally changed our lives."

—Tina B, mother of a three-year-old

"The shell that was around him has dropped off, and he has light."

—Mary S, mother of a six-year-old

"It's a lot easier than I thought it was going to be. At first I was like, 'oh, my gosh! I'm not ready for this.' But it's not hard. It really isn't!"

—Alice M, mother of a five-year-old

"One day he just put his arms around me and said 'I love you mommy.' You could see in his eyes he understood love."

—Linda L, mother of a three-year-old

"When we believed that autism was permanent and unchangeable, we wouldn't have thought of trying to improve it. Now we believe autism is treatable. We do the massage every day."

—Deb M, mother of a six-year-old

"We started looking for sensory help and had no idea that other areas like speech and language would also improve. I had no clue. I'm just dumbfounded by the whole thing!"

—Bonnie L, mother of a five-year-old

"Now he wants to brush his own teeth, he lets us brush his hair; I even checked him for head lice last night. When I started he said, 'don't hurt me.' After a moment he said, 'that doesn't hurt.' I was checking him like any other kid and he didn't scream or fight."

—Keith R, father of a four-year-old

of related interest

Therapeutic Massage and Bodywork for Autism Spectrum Disorders
A Guide for Parents and Caregivers
Virginia S. Cowen
ISBN 978 1 84819 049 8

Six Healing Sounds with Lisa and Ted
Qigong for Children
Lisa Spillane
ISBN 978 1 84819 051 1

Yoga Therapy for Every Special Child
Meeting Needs in a Natural Setting
Nancy Williams
Illustrated by Leslie White
ISBN 978 1 84819 027 6

Yoga for Children with Autism Spectrum Disorders
A Step-by-Step Guide for Parents and Caregivers
Dion E. Betts and Stacey W. Betts
Forewords by Louise Goldberg, Registered Yoga Teacher, and Joshua S. Betts
ISBN 978 1 84310 817 7

Integrated Yoga
Yoga with a Sensory Integrative Approach
Nicole Cuomo
ISBN 978 1 84310 862 7

Qigong
Massage

for Your Child with Autism

A Home Program from Chinese Medicine

Louisa Silva

Foreword by Dr. Anita Cignolini

SINGING
DRAGON

LONDON AND PHILADELPHIA

The lines from "i thank You God for this most amazing" on page 6 are used by kind permission of Liveright Publishing Corporation. Copyright © 1950, 1978, 1991 by the Trustees for the E. E. Cummings Trust. Copyright © 1979 by George James Firmage, from *Complete Poems: 1904–1962* by E. E. Cummings, edited by George J. Firmage.

This edition published in 2011
by Singing Dragon
an imprint of Jessica Kingsley Publishers
73 Collier Street
London N1 9BE, UK
and
400 Market Street, Suite 400
Philadelphia, PA 19106, USA

www.singingdragon.com

First published by Guan Yin Press in 2010

Copyright © Louisa Silva 2010 and 2011
Foreword copyright © Anita Cignolini 2011
Cover based on a design by Rob Larsen

Library of Congress Cataloging in Publication Data
A CIP catalog record for this book is available from the Library of Congress

British Library Cataloguing in Publication Data
A CIP catalogue record for this book is available from the British Library

ISBN 978-1-78592-982-3
eISBN 978-0-85701-041-4

Printed and bound in Great Britain

To Aaron, Wendy, and Matt, who inspired this book, and to all the families who will some day read it

now the ears of my ears awake and now the eyes
of my eyes are opened.

e.e. cummings

CONTENTS

A Note on Vocabulary

We live in a world rich in definitions of "family." In writing this book, we refer to the primary caregiver as "parent" and the second adult most connected to the child as "parent" or sometimes "partner." We see in these words the connection that is unique to children and the particular adult(s) who, in the parental role, shelter, love, nourish, and teach them. A parent who is the only adult in the household should not despair. A second adult is helpful, but not required. Forge ahead anyway.

FOREWORD

I had the pleasure to teach Dr. Silva and work with her on the first research studies applying scientific standards to test the effectiveness of my qigong massage treatment for young children with autism. My work in the field of Chinese Classical Medicine began in the early seventies and included many periods of intense study and research in academies and universities in China. Over the years I developed a rich knowledge of the theory and its fascinating clinical applications little known in the West. During my practice in both Europe and the United States I had the opportunity to apply my knowledge to the treatment of children, and was the first doctor to do it outside of China. My work in these years led to an ever greater appreciation for the need to discover how to apply these methods to the growing population of children suffering from disturbances with Autism Spectrum Disorders. I worked to develop the theory and intervention protocol that is now known as the Cignolini Method. This was the methodology for which Dr. Silva and I first published research showing effectiveness for young children with autism. In her work to bring qigong massage to early intervention therapists, and directly to parents, Dr. Silva has since adapted and expanded my original methodology. I am pleased to accept her gratitude to me for being her professor of Chinese medicine, and endorse her work in bringing this precious knowledge to the many families that it can benefit.

Dr. Anita Cignolini, MD
Palermo
March 2011

PREFACE

Welcome!

In picking up this book, you have taken the first step in embarking on a magnificent journey, one that can have a significant positive impact on your child's struggle with autism and on your family. For centuries, Chinese medicine has treated children's illnesses with massage and diet. On the pages that follow, you will learn a simple 15-minute massage program to help your child's nervous system open up and thus help him become more aware of the world around him. Given every day for five months, it will reduce the symptoms of autism and improve sleep and digestion. The research shows that when combined with some simple dietary recommendations and common-sense protection from toxins, this program can strengthen the body, mind, and emotions of your child, and set him or her on a more normal developmental path.

Chinese medicine offers many different home massage programs for different children's illnesses and disabilities. This book describes a program that has been shown in rigorous scientific research to significantly diminish the effects of autism in children age six and under. It is important to say that it is not appropriate for children with other serious medical conditions, such as uncontrolled seizures or severe emotional disturbances, nor has it been proven to be the optimum massage treatment for older children with autism. But as for the children under six with autism or sensory problems, parents who give their children this simple, daily, 15-minute massage reported that within a few months mood and behavior was better, social and language skills increased, and the stress of caring for their child with autism was significantly diminished.

Our earliest research used trained practitioners who worked intimately with the families who participated in the studies. This work occurred over a prolonged training and included 20 subsequent visits where the practitioner administered the massage, in addition to the daily massage done by the parents at home. We were delighted with the results. The children in the study showed significant improvement. We then launched studies in which the parents had training and coaching from a trainer, but did the massage themselves. Again, we had exciting positive results. Over the years, we have perfected the specifics and continually moved toward creating a program that enables parents—once they understand the massage and make the commitment to follow through—to achieve, on their own, the same positive results the families in our first studies enjoyed.

Learning something new has a natural learning curve. We had to put a lot of information in this book to make it a complete resource, so you might feel a little overwhelmed by the time you close the book the first time. Hang in there; it gets easier. The program is actually surprisingly simple. For most people who pick up this book, the concepts behind qigong massage are entirely foreign. It might take a while to get there, but, if you stick with it, it will become second nature.

We are so excited to be able to make this program available to everyone. Before this handbook, we were only able to help families in our geographic area. Now, we can offer it to you wherever you are. We wish you the best success. If you have problems or questions, there is contact information in the Additional Resources on page 137. Write us, or email us or check our website. We want to help you and your child unlock his or her potential and join in all the world has to offer.

Note

All of the studies discussed in this book were done on children up to the age of six. While we have anecdotal evidence to show that the massage works for older children, we have no empirical evidence to support any claims in that regard. In general, our expectations of the over-six group would be that the massage would be most successful with smaller, younger children.

The online materials can be found at www.jkp.com/voucher using the code QIGONGMASSAGE.

INTRODUCTION

Making the Most of This Book

The treatment described in this book has had *proven* results in children with autism under six years of age. This success came from parents who were able to learn the massage, get it into their child's routine, and give it every day for five months. As the weeks passed, the children improved. Children started to ask for their massage and parents came to enjoy it as a close time with their child.

Still more can be gained, however, by parents who work with their child's responses *during* the massage. The more the parent adjusts the massage to their child's body language during the massage, the better the results. In our studies, we had trainers involved to ensure that the parents had every chance to most fully understand how to attune the massage to their child's changing responses. These were hands-on professionals who checked in with the parents regularly to coach them and to improve their techniques.

While we have made every attempt to describe the steps clearly in this book, most people who will be using it will not have the benefit of a professional to guide them. For this reason, we strongly recommend that you gather some other parents of children who have autism into a massage group so that you can learn the steps together, share information and discoveries, and give feedback to one another as you hone your skills. It will also help you stick with it through the sometimes difficult first weeks until you begin to see and recognize tangible results.

You probably already know other parents of children on the autism spectrum through your early intervention program. If a group of five or six families doesn't come to mind immediately, ask your early intervention specialist to suggest some families. Also check any online support groups to which you might belong.

Having specific goals for such a group is important. Of course, every group will create their own goals and culture. You might form the group to achieve a few stated objectives and then disband. Or you might find new friends who can share this journey with you, providing help and support in ways that far surpass the scope of this program.

Here are the initial goals we suggest:

- Bring the group together initially to watch the videos together. Set this date whether people have read this book or not. Try to arrange it as an adults-only gathering so people can pay close attention to the videos.

- Everyone should have a copy of the book. It helps if people have watched the videos and/or read the book prior to coming, but it shouldn't be a requirement.

- Take a moment for each parent or couple to turn to Appendix C and record the three specific improvements in their child that would be the most helpful or meaningful for their family (e.g. sleeps through the night, responds to her name, aggression subsides).

- After watching all 12 massage movements in the online materials to see the flow of it, watch the first two movements again and then break into groups of three or four to practice giving the massage to one another. Refer to the Movement Chart on page 141–142. Then watch the next two movements, practice those, and continue watching and practicing two at a time, until you've practiced all 12.

- It is best if everyone gets to give the massage and receive the massage at least once. For the sake of social comfort, you can adapt the massage (patting the air above the chest or buttocks, for example) for this activity. The others in the group should watch and give feedback, using the Movement Troubleshooting Checklist in Appendix A as a guide.

- Gather together after the practice time to compare notes about what was learned or observed and to ask questions if they came up. Trade contact information so you can talk over questions or observations later.

- Then, meet in a week as a group or in pairs, to demonstrate the massage again for one another; again using the Movement Troubleshooting Checklist and comparing against the Movement Chart to be sure that the movements are being done correctly.

- Take a moment to mark your calendars to remind yourselves to reread the book or go through the Movement Troubleshooting Checklist again.

This practice and feedback will help ensure that the participants are leaving prepared to start practicing on their own. Everyone should plan to practice at home, with a partner or typically developing child, before beginning with their child. They should also read the entire handbook before they begin, paying careful attention to the step-by-step instructions in Chapter 4. If they go only with the experience from the parent meeting, they will miss much of the material that is critical to their success.

Subsequent meetings, once or twice a month, are helpful because those who are seeing results early will inspire others to continue. Also, on those days when you are tempted to skip the massage, knowing that you will be meeting again and reporting whether you are doing the massage daily will help you keep going and keep you learning from others' experience and insight. Regular contact between group members outside of the meetings can be very helpful and provide support.

Every child will respond differently to the massage program and will progress at her own pace

---

There will be lots for the group to share, and you will be continually reminded of something you already know: every child is different. Everyone should fill out a Developmental Checklist from the QSTI.org website. A much-abbreviated version of it is in Appendix C. The measure of progress is not how fast or slow your child improves compared to someone else, but to where your child began.

Chapter 1

An Eastern Explanation and Treatment for Autism

The phrase "to be comfortable in your own skin" is an old one, one that exists in many languages. It tells us something about how we function as human beings and how we relate to one another. A person who is comfortable in his own skin is both comfortable with himself, and relaxed in company. She is easy to talk to and talks easily to others. The idea of being comfortable with ourselves and others includes all of our senses, because we use our senses to know ourselves and to relate to others. Children on the autism spectrum don't feel comfortable in their skin. Massage is a way to give that comfort back to them.

Qi, our life energy

The massage you are about to learn is based on ancient Chinese ideas about energy and how it works in the body. To do the massage well, you need to learn some of the concepts behind it. You'll learn to use the word "qi" (chee) or energy, and a related word "qigong" (chee-gong), working with energy using exercises or massage. When we say we are low in energy, it means we don't have much qi-energy. Qigong helps us improve the quality and quantity of our qi-energy.

One of the best tools qigong gives us is a way to improve our circulation. This is because qi-energy and circulation are linked. When we improve our energy, we improve our circulation.

The particular form of qigong massage that we recommend is called Qigong Sensory Training, or QST for short. It is one of hundreds of possible massage routines used by Chinese medicine to treat illness, and it is specific for autism and sensory problems.

In the West, the concept of "life energy" is somewhat mysterious and nebulous. Not so in China, where our physical energy has been understood for three thousand years. If a person needs to improve her overall energy and circulation, there are qigong exercises and massages for that. If he needs to improve his digestion, there are different qigong exercises and a particular diet.

Just like the earth has an electromagnetic field, so do we. Our energy circulates continually in this field from the top of our head, down the outside of our body to our hands and our feet, and then back up the inside of our body to our head again. As our energy flows, it helps our blood circulate into our tissues.

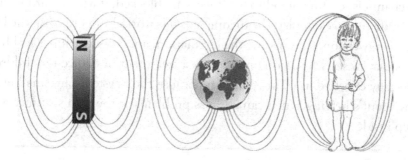

In health, we have plenty of energy and good circulation. In illness, we have problems with our energy and circulation. What parents need to learn about qigong massage isn't complicated and, in fact, you'll be surprised at how well it explains much of what you've seen and experienced with autism.

We've treated many children with autism whose parents now use concepts about energy and circulation daily to help their children. And so, although the ideas might be new to many, they work, regardless of whether we understand and recognize them or not. Our children's bodies behave in the way the Chinese describe. Once you learn how to see their bodies in terms of energy and circulation, the massage becomes reassuringly predictable.

In this book, we do our best to give you clear, simple instructions for giving the massage, and what signs to look for in your child. After you've done the massage a number of times, you will recognize that your child is starting to react just as we have described, and the instructions will make more sense to you. If your child doesn't react as predicted, there will be a reason for it, and answers that we can search for.

Energy channels

Once you understand the idea that our bodies have an energy field, the next idea to grasp is that within our energy field there is a system of energy channels. You might be surprised to learn that there is a map of these energy channels, and that Chinese medicine has known about this map for thousands of years. They are like a system of rivers flowing north–south, and east–west, bringing life energy and blood to all our tissues. We use this map to understand *where* the problems are when we do qigong massage.

As the energy flows through the channels, it sends blood in and out of the little capillaries that deliver nutrients to the tissues. If the channel is blocked in an area, that area will have poor circulation and won't feel right. If, for example, the circulation is blocked to your child's scalp, it will be difficult to cut his hair. If the channels sending blood to his fingers are blocked, it will be hard to cut his nails. In these two examples, the qigong massage works by opening up the blocks in the energy channels, restoring the circulation, and making things feel better.

It is easy to see why qigong massage is a treatment of choice for children. It is especially effective in young children because their systems are small enough that a parent's healing touch can address problems at the skin's surface as well as deep inside.

"In terms of what they said in the trainings about the things he has difficulty with—everything improved exactly like the training said it would, especially his finger sensitivities and his verbal abilities. I can even cut his nails now. I personally like the qigong because it is not anything that is scary or invasive, it is just a massage." (Tom's dad)

The three energy "sources"

There is one more concept from Chinese medicine that will help us understand qigong massage, and our children's reactions to it. It has to do with the *sources* of the electromagnetic activity in our bodies. Just like the Earth's electromagnetic field has a *source*—its molten iron core—so our electromagnetic field also has a source. Actually, we have three sources. Deep in the head, chest, and abdomen are areas of concentrated energy, which the Chinese call *dantien*. These are the deep sources and reserves for our mental, emotional, and physical energy.

Although we don't conceptualize these energy sources in the West specifically, nor do we map them as the Chinese do, we do differentiate between our physical, emotional, and mental energy. We have a sense that our mental energy centers in our head, our emotional energy centers in our heart, and our physical energy centers in our gut. We are aware when our reserves are tapped, and we become mentally, emotionally, or physically run down. Chinese medicine teaches that when we have been ill for some time, eventually we draw down our reserves, and they become depleted and empty. It offers us a way to replenish and restore the sources of our energy—qigong exercises and massage. During the five months of this program, parents will be doing this for their children by placing a gentle hand over their heart, forehead, and lower belly during the massage. Children, likewise, will be drawing their parent's hands to these areas, asking them without words to help fill them up.

When it comes to understanding energy, "seeing is believing." We don't want you to take anything on faith, so just keep an open mind, follow our instructions, observe your child, and see for yourself.

One of the best things about a parent giving their child qigong massage is that a parent and child share the same energy. When a parent gives a child energy, it is like giving them a blood transfusion with perfectly matched blood—it is exactly what they need without side-effects. This, and the love a parent shares with their child, can make qigong massage given by the parent more effective than qigong massage given by a professional. This is one situation where you really can be the best doctor for your child.

Energy and autism

Let's try to understand more about what your child's physical energy has to do with her autism by looking at a couple of different forms of autism. In the regressive form of autism, for example, a child develops normally until somewhere in her second year, and then suddenly loses speech and eye contact and regresses into autism. Alternatively, in the non-regressive form, she may be going along developing normally, when at a certain moment, her development just peters out. What happened to her energy? What was her energy like when she was growing normally? What happened when she stopped?

Chinese medicine would say that before your child got autism, her energy flowed freely and abundantly down from the top of her head to the tips of her fingers and toes, keeping her head clear, her eyes and ears open, her fingers and toes comfortable, and sending blood into all her tissues and organs to keep her healthy and developing normally.

In any situation where we have illness or pain in our body, Chinese medicine makes the diagnosis of a block in our energy and circulation, and then gives treatment to open up the block and restore circulation. It pays particular attention to where the block is.

In both of our examples, regressive and non-regressive, when our little girl developed autism, her energy and circulation became blocked in her head and neck. Her head was no longer clear, her eyes and ears no longer worked together. Downstream of the block, the circulation to her fingers and toes was diminished, and her skin stopped feeling normal. The circulation to her brain and organs suffered, and her development slowed down. Terrible though this is, these blocks can be reversed.

In autism, there are many blocks in the channels through which qi-energy travels—especially in the areas where the senses open to the world around us. Because these conditions prevent the senses from working properly, the child can't receive accurate information about the world around him. These different sensory problems result in troubling behaviors and a limited ability to learn and socialize. Depending on the blocks and the degree of emptiness in their energy sources and reservoirs, children with autism lack the robust health the typical child exhibits.

- Qi means energy.

- Gong means skilled work or craft.

- Qigong means working with energy.

The removal of these blocks and the filling of the channels with qi-energy is at the heart of what this qigong massage accomplishes. As you progress through these pages, you'll learn to recognize blocks when you see them. And you'll learn techniques for knowing when and how to help your child fill the places that are empty of qi-energy and blood. We'll discuss the causes of these blocks in a later chapter, but the exciting thing is that qigong massage removes these sensory blocks very well. And through the massage, many parents have already been able to help their child open up to the world.

Take a moment to visualize a river that is watering a vast, verdant delta. If you dam up the river, parts of the downstream environment will begin to wither. Things might still live there, but growth will be impeded and the area will not flourish. The energy system that enables a rich flow of blood to the body is similar. Once we remove the dams and refresh the reservoirs in a child who is struggling with autism, normal function can return in many areas.

Remember that autism is not a genetic disease in the way Down syndrome is; the manifestations of the disease are not fixed. In other words, the diagnosis in the case of autism is merely a snapshot in time of where your child registers as being behind on his developmental milestones. As you will see, he can catch up. And the tools are, literally, at hand.

We have found that it takes about two months for the massage to become automatic for parents, and for them to become fully comfortable with the concepts we present in the following pages. By this time, the massage is typically a relaxing, enjoyable time of the day for both parent and child. In our research, parents who complete the five-month program report a significant reduction in stress levels across the board as autistic behaviors abate in their child. If you persevere and get past the initial learning curve, you can have these kinds of outcomes, too.

Treating the causes of autism with qigong massage

Chinese medicine says, "for every physical illness there is a problem with our energy channels." For example, if you have a pain in your shoulder, and can't lift your arm, we would look for a block in your channels where they run through the shoulder. Once we found the sore spot, we would carefully massage and pat it down towards your hand. It would be like combing the tangles out of long hair. We would keep going until we got the tangle out.

So one of our first questions in autism is, "Where are the blocks?" We want to find them, and work them out. Whether you believe in these blocks or not, if you *try* to massage them out, you will *see* them melt away.

Qigong massage works differently than ordinary massage. It follows the energy channels instead of the lymph drainage, it provides lasting improvement instead of temporary relief, and, because it works on energy, it addresses the whole person instead of the separate parts.

One of the main practical differences you will learn over and over again, as you learn the massage, is that the direction of the strokes in qigong massage is very important; we always move down from the head to the hands and feet.

The first step to working with your child using qigong is to have a broad understanding of the autism symptoms you see in relation to how the massage will address them. This general understanding is important so you can more easily understand your child's responses during the massage and appropriately respond to them.

Treating the symptoms of autism with qigong massage
Sensory problems

Research shows that behind the developmental delay seen in children with autism lies a sensory nervous system that is out of balance—the child's skin, eyes, ears, and nose simply don't perceive his own body and the events of family life in the same way that the rest of the family does. Children with autism might not notice if someone speaks to them. Their perception of gentle touch and of pain can be out of kilter on different parts of their body. Things that should feel good (e.g. holding hands, hugs from grandparents) don't feel good, and things that should hurt (e.g. cuts, scrapes, burns) don't hurt. In the end, the positive reinforcement that comes from feeling good when we are with our loved ones isn't the same and social interaction doesn't come naturally.

Because the senses are out of balance, they don't work together. It is hard for a child with autism to pick out a human voice and a human face from all the other sights and sounds. And then it is hard to coordinate turning her head with looking at and listening to someone. That is why the hallmark of autism is *not making eye contact*—her sensory nervous system isn't working properly.

Eye contact is critical to communication. Trying to communicate without eye contact is like talking through a telephone line that keeps breaking up—it's really hard to get the information across. With no eye contact, communication is an uphill battle. No wonder it is hard for children with autism to learn language and social skills. How do we help his sensory nervous system so he can connect naturally with the people in his world?

Qigong massage and sensory problems

The qigong massage described in this book restores the normal feeling of pain and pleasure to all five senses. Now the sensory information from the skin, eyes, and ears stops being contradictory and starts fitting together. The senses work together and the child can make sense of what the people in his world are doing. He is curious and begins to make eye contact and tune in.

Once the senses are working better, many of the symptoms of autism begin to abate. It is easier for the child to focus and pay attention to what is going on around her. With her senses no longer overloaded all the time, the child is more relaxed about participating in social situations. It becomes fun to play with other children, and social learning is free to come naturally out of day-to-day experiences.

Stress and relaxation problems

The human nervous system is set up to trigger two opposite states of being: stress and relaxation. The first state is triggered in response to discomfort, and is why the baby cries when she is hungry or wet. It is under the control of the *sympathetic nervous system*. The second state is triggered by the pleasure of food and comfort and is where she spends most of her time. When she is relaxed, she opens up the world around her. Because she is a young mammal, her security and comfort come with her social group, and she has the ability to relax and enjoy togetherness. The relaxed state allows her to bond with her family, digest her food properly, be social with others, and fall asleep at night. This state is under the control of the *parasympathetic nervous system.*

So what happens in autism? Children with autism don't tolerate change well. Day-to-day changes are difficult to cope with and even a small change in the routine can trigger a meltdown. Research shows that this is because in autism the parasympathetic nervous system is underactive. Without its calming influence, the child's nervous system is easily tipped towards stress, and does not know how to de-stress.

From the moment of birth, we experience many episodes of stress, and have to learn from our parents how to calm down. When a baby has a need that is not immediately met, his stress doesn't automatically go away when his need is fulfilled. He needs to be held and soothed by the parent. This triggers the parasympathetic nervous system, and he relaxes again. As he gets older, he learns to soothe himself, and to trigger his own parasympathetic nervous system. He tolerates change better, and once he can communicate his needs and wants more clearly, he can change the situation to meet his needs. By the time he is in preschool, he is starting to be able to stay calm and open in social settings where there is an amazing amount of change and activity going on around him.

Often children with autism did not learn to self-soothe in the first year of life, and small changes in the routine can easily trigger tantrums. The child is difficult to calm and so the tantrums can be both long and loud. The stress impacts everyone in the family. Parents also have to deal with uninformed outsiders commenting on the child's "bad behavior." Public situations like the grocery store, where the child has to respond to even more stimulation and change, most of which the parents can't control, become especially stressful for parents.

Qigong massage and stress and relaxation problems

Qigong massage awakens and stimulates the self-soothing mechanisms in the body, enabling the child to participate in family and school life without becoming overwhelmed. With the ability to self-soothe, she can better handle the changes and transitions of her daily life. As the massage helps her to be more comfortable in her skin, she learns to recognize and communicate her needs more clearly and the stress response is triggered less frequently. Eventually, the self-soothing abilities become embedded in her nervous system and she learns to regulate her emotions and stress levels so that they are appropriate to her needs and the situation around her.

Repetitive and self-injurious behaviors

In our work with children who have autism, we see *self-injurious* behaviors such as self-biting, pinching, and head-banging as a response on the part of the child to "wrong" sensory information coming in. While self-injurious behavior is an attempt to muffle or stop the sensation, repetitive motions, such as rocking, are an attempt to self-soothe.

Other *repetitive* motions, such as repeatedly turning the light switch on and off or lining up toys, are like a phonograph needle stuck in the groove of an old LP record. By practicing tasks, very young children learn to understand and manipulate predictable elements of their world. They practice through repetition until they've mastered the skill and then they move on to the next thing. Children with autism engage in the first part of this, but, because their senses are impaired, they can't really pay attention to what they experience. So they never learn enough to abandon the behavior and move on to the next step.

Qigong massage and repetitive or self-injurious behaviors

Once the sensory nervous system comes back to normal, the uncomfortable sensory messages cease, and the self-injury response stops. And, because the senses open up and the child starts to notice what he is doing during the repetitive behaviors, he learns from what he is doing, and progresses on to the next step. So, even though he is delayed according to a typical timetable, the child is no longer stuck in the same groove.

Tantrums and meltdowns

All parents expect a few tantrums from their toddler, but parents of children with autism often distinguish between tantrums—which in autism are typically more frequent, longer, and more easily triggered—and meltdowns. To the parents of a child with autism, a meltdown is a situation in which screaming and hitting escalates, the child is usually on the floor, and it takes a long time for the tantrum to dissipate.

Parents of toddlers learn to recognize the signs of a pending meltdown in their child and put the child down for a nap or otherwise anticipate their child's needs according to what they perceive is wearing him down. The typically growing child learns to tolerate longer periods of discomfort and adapts to not having his needs met immediately. For the child with autism, the world is already taxing his system far beyond the experience of the normal child. He might "hit the wall" more suddenly, and because the self-soothing mechanisms are not functioning well, he has little ability to fend off the meltdown himself.

Qigong massage and tantrums and meltdowns

The movements that promote self-soothing are critical parts of the qigong massage program. As the child's nervous system begins to learn to calm itself instead of being overwhelmed by stress, the meltdowns become less frequent. Additionally, because the child begins to learn more about his world and to recognize and communicate his needs better, the situations that caused him to have a meltdown previously cease to be problems.

A few months into the massage program, when parents can take a deep breath and reflect, there is often a tremendous sense of liberation and joy to realize that this behavior that has been such an exhausting part of daily life is abating. Does this mean that tantrums and meltdowns will cease completely? Of course not. The child still has to grow through all the stages of development, including those in which a meltdown is going to happen even for a typically developing child. The difference is that the meltdowns are much less frequent and the parents can now respond to them as they would with a healthy, albeit younger, child.

Aggressive behaviors

Aggressive behavior is possibly the most stressful for families, especially if the child with autism is aggressive with a younger sibling. As in other troubling behaviors common to autism, aggression is a result of the nervous system being more tipped towards stress—the "fight or flight" state typical of the sympathetic nervous system—than relaxation. A second factor that triggers aggressive behavior is exposure to toxins. Children with autism have an immature detoxification system, and may not be able to handle certain foods or products in the home that are harmless to the rest of the family. There is more about this in Chapter 9. An exposure to a toxin can result in unusual or aggressive behavior. For some children, the triggers can be fairly easy to spot, and, once eliminated from the child's environment, the aggression can abate. Examples of substances that can trigger aggression are things like markers (switch to crayons!) or processed food with red dye.

Qigong massage and aggressive behaviors

The qigong massage addresses three underlying problems that cause aggression in children with autism. The first is the ability to self-soothe. A child who can properly self-soothe will be triggered to aggressive behavior less frequently. As the child spends more time in the relaxed, open, learning state, the "fight" response won't be part of an ever-present state of being for the child. The aggression might continue for a while, but the number of instances should abate significantly over the months of the massage. Also, as the child is better able to understand what is happening around him and to communicate his needs, his frustration levels will go down, and his tendency to trigger into aggression should diminish.

The second effect of the massage is in the reduction of toxins in the body. While eliminating toxins in the environment can also help significantly, the qigong massage boosts and balances the digestive system so the child can clear the toxins he is already holding in his body and better process new ones coming in. Soon after beginning the massage, you should see one or more smelly green poops. This is evidence that the body is finally able to process and shed these foreign substances that can have a hand in fostering aggressive responses.

The third contribution the massage can make toward reducing aggression is that, as the senses open and the child's body becomes more balanced, he begins to develop empathy. For the child who did not feel pain previously, these sensory openings are critical: without the ability to feel pain, he cannot understand pain in others. When a child cries for the first time after injuring himself, the door to acquiring empathy has opened and the child can begin to learn that aggressive behavior can hurt others.

Sleep problems

Children with autism have a high prevalence of sleep problems including sleeping very little, great difficulty falling asleep, being awake for long periods of time at night, nightmares and night screaming. Easing into sleep and staying asleep is regulated by the nervous system. Because the calming, relaxed, open state of the parasympathetic nervous system is not the dominant state in most children with autism, the ability to wind down to sleep and stay asleep are not readily at hand.

Sleep problems make it harder for the child to cope with daily life because she is not rested, so the symptoms of autism are amplified. Children's sleep problems also dramatically impact the parents' stress levels and quality of life. Parents of children with autism can be severely and chronically sleep-deprived, which only adds to the difficulties of caring for the child on top of coping with all the other demands of home and work.

Qigong massage and sleep problems

Our research has shown qigong massage is helpful in improving all manner of sleep problems in children who have autism, within the first few months of implementation. The most common time of day parents in our studies chose to give the massage was at bedtime. They consistently report that the massage becomes a relaxing part of the bedtime routine, enjoyed by both the parent and the child, often ending with the child being asleep within minutes.

Digestive problems

Children with autism commonly have an array of digestive problems that can include diarrhea, constipation, poor appetite, and/or food allergies. Young children require specific nutrients to support the needs of the developing brain and body. If a child is eating a severely limited diet, he might not be getting the necessary nutrients for brain development. Or, if she is eating nutritious foods but has diarrhea, she might not be absorbing the nutrients she needs. In either situation, growth and development may be hindered.

For children who already have developmental delay, this is a double-whammy, because their digestive problems create a further barrier to learning and health that can lead to a downward spiral in their condition. Because the nervous system regulates digestion, it is little wonder that children who have a disrupted nervous system will have problems in this area. After all, when somebody is wound up and on full alert, she is in no position to relish a meal. Nor will her body digest it well.

Because this is a common state for children with autism, getting nutritional value from food is a chronic challenge for their bodies. Add to that the probability that their sense of taste and their sensations of texture are likely to also be disrupted and it can be hard to get nutritious food into their system. As they restrict their diet to fewer and fewer foods, the likelihood of developing food allergies increases.

Qigong massage and digestive problems

The digestive problems of children in our studies consistently abated as the digestive systems became stronger and the choice of food widened. Diarrhea and constipation resolved and appetite improved. As their bodies began to be fully nourished, their intellect was able to open to the new, more accurate, sensory input they were suddenly receiving. Their bodies and minds began to grow naturally.

If a child has food allergies, the massage not only makes it easier for her to handle the allergies by helping her to better eliminate toxins from her system, but it also broadens the array of foods she'll eat. Because we often crave the foods to which we are allergic, the improvement of appetite resulting from the massage makes it easier to sort out the foods to which a child is reacting and to eliminate them for a time. (For more information about diet and food allergies see Chapter 10.)

Chapter 2

Is the QST Home Program Right for You and Your Child?

The QST Home Program is a treatment that you will be giving your child at home. It is important to make sure it is the *right* treatment for you and your child. Our definition of a right treatment to put in parents' hands is a treatment that is safe, effective, non-invasive, and can be successfully carried out by parents without taking too much of their time and energy. All treatments take a parent's time and energy, but some are much more burdensome than others. As you are researching and coming to your decision, here are some questions that will help you decide.

For whom is the QST Home Program recommended?

Our research has shown that the home program is safe and effective for children with uncomplicated autism who are six years and under, and are not undergoing other intensive medical treatments.

Who is the QST Home Program not recommended for and why?

- *Children who have active seizures.* If a child has an active seizure disorder that is not controlled on medication, then the gentle qigong tapping on the head can actually trigger a seizure. These children should not receive qigong massage unless it is under the direction of a Chinese medicine physician.

- *Children who have other complicated medical and emotional conditions.* The QST Home Program is just one of many possible massage programs, and is tailored for uncomplicated autism and sensory problems. Children with other severe physical or emotional problems would need a different home program, and it should be individually tailored to them by a Chinese medicine physician.

- *Children who are going through a lot of medication changes.* The success of qigong massage comes when the parent can read and respond to the child's cues during massage. While a child is going through a lot of medication changes, the medication is affecting the child's body, and this makes it difficult to know whether the child is reacting to the massage or reacting to the medication. Some strong medications like Tegretol or Risperdal tend to block the effect of the qigong massage altogether. In general, it is better to wait until the child is stabilized on medication before beginning the home program.

- *Children going through chelation therapy.* Chelation is a very strong treatment. It releases toxins and can cause regressions in behavior. It is much better not to mix qigong with chelation as the chelation process makes it far too difficult for the parent to tune the massage to the child.

Can I give the massage to my other typically developing children?
Absolutely.

Can I give the massage to my older child who has autism?
The research is not in on this one. You will have to decide for yourself and do what is comfortable for you. Some of our parents have given the massage to their older children and had great results. Others couldn't get past the initial difficulties and the child's rejection of touch. We hope to do a research study with older children so we can encounter the problems systematically and be in a position to offer strategies.

Can I give the massage to other children with other medical conditions?
Better not. We are currently researching a home massage program for cerebral palsy and Down syndrome. Keep checking our website. If the study results are good, we will post the information there as soon as we have it.

Chapter 3

GETTING READY TO GIVE THE HOME PROGRAM

Now that you have decided that the QST Home Program is right for your child, a number of questions go through your mind: Is it affordable? Is it hard to learn? Is it time-consuming to give? Luckily for parents, qigong massage is parent-friendly on all these counts. It can be given in the home at no expense and it takes only 15 minutes a day. Qigong massage is among the least invasive of all the autism treatments—it involves neither medication nor lengthy therapy—and research shows that, when done correctly, it is both safe and effective.

Thousands of years of experience with qigong massage in China show that the younger the child is, the more effective it is. That is why we strongly recommend it as a first-line early intervention as soon as a diagnosis of autism is suspected.

Through the past decade of working with parents, we have found that the success of this program depends on one main thing: *the parents get the massage into the daily routine and keep it there for five months.* It is really that simple. The massage works, you just have to do it! Once they get over the hump of learning the massage and getting their children over their worst sensory problems, we have found that parents, as well as children, enjoy the massage, and it is not difficult to keep it in the routine.

Massaging your child strengthens the bond between you, and when see you are helping him to overcome some of the obstacles in his path, you will feel great satisfaction in your job as a parent.

Following are some of the most common questions we hear as parents get ready to start the home program.

Who should do the massage?

Any adult family member *who is emotionally connected to the child* can learn to give the massage. In fact, it is best for at least two family members to learn how to give it. That way if one person is too tired or is unavailable, the child needn't miss out on the help and support the massage offers.

When should I do the massage?

Bedtime is a great time to give the massage because it helps the child to quiet down to sleep, but before or after school or before nap time might work better for you. The important thing is to get it into the daily routine at a time that supports your ability to get it done. After a while, your child will expect it and ask for it.

Where should I do the massage?

You don't need any special mats or tables to do qigong massage, but it will be best if you can find a comfortable spot that you can use most days—a bed, a couch, or even the floor with a comforting blanket and pillow. It is up to you and your child what will work best for the two of you. Ideally, it is a place where the child has the best chance of relaxing and where you can comfortably get to both sides of his body. This will make it easier for you to make the massage part of your daily routine.

How long do I need to continue the program?

The massage is like a calming and balancing medicine. You should give it daily for at least five months. Then you can decide whether to continue. We recommend that you fill out the checklists in the Appendices before you start, and again at five months. This will help you measure the progress your child has made, and give you some benchmarks to decide how long to continue. Many parents keep going for a year or two, because they see that the massage keeps their child on track, and without it, their child's progress slips a bit.

Are there times when I shouldn't give the massage?

Giving qigong massage requires some extra energy of the person who is giving it. Everyone has days when they have nothing left to give, either because they are too stressed, too tired, are getting sick, or are in too bad a mood. *If you are sick, angry, or exhausted, do not give the massage.* Going through the motions with a negative feeling will not help your child—our children feel our emotions. Ask another family member to do it. If nobody else is available, it is better to take the day off and wait for a new day when you are feeling better. Feeling calm, open, and positive yourself is a vital part of the treatment. If you are mildly stressed or somewhat tired, however, giving the massage will help you calm down and relax, and then both you and your child will feel better.

What if my child isn't feeling well?

You will need to play this one by ear. If your child is aching all over with the flu, for example, the massage would be uncomfortable and not a good idea, but if your child has something minor like a cold or upset stomach, the massage can help him get over it much faster.

What if I make mistakes?

Parents are often afraid of making mistakes. The big mistakes are obvious, and you aren't going to make them: to be rough with your child, to give the massage when you are angry, or massage upward towards the head. If you study this book and online materials, remain gentle and calm, and follow the qigong movements downwards from the head towards the hands and feet, you won't harm your child. It's normal to feel uncertain of your abilities when you are learning something new. But, as you do the massage every day, your skills at reading your child's body language will get better, and your child will start asking you for the massage.

How will I ever remember all 12 movements?

It might feel like 12 separate movements is a lot to learn, but you'll soon find that you can move through the movements with ease. They become second nature. In fact, over time, children learn the parts of the massage and ask for them.

Until then, here's some help: there is a Movement Chart at the back of this book (see page 141–142). While it doesn't teach you what you need to know about the movements, once you have worked through this book, it is an excellent quick reference sheet. You might like to turn to this page and follow along on the chart now.

First, notice that the movements fall naturally into four groups:

1. The first two movements focus on the full length of the body down the back. Then you turn the child over, and the third movement focuses on the full length of the sides of the body.

2. The second group of three movements focuses on the energy moving from the head, down the arms, and into the fingertips.

3. The third group, which consists of Movements 7 and 8, focuses on the chest and abdomen.

4. The fourth group of four movements is done with the legs, toes, and feet.

So, it's really very easy. Start with the whole body, take care of the arms, address the torso, and finish with the legs and feet. Everything is moving *down* the body.

Which movements do what?

By starting at the top of the head with Movements 1, 2, and 3, you are opening your child's awareness of the world around her. It usually takes some weeks before she can lie quietly on her belly as you do the movements, but by the time that has happened, you will see that you've accomplished a great deal in helping her to be more aware of her surroundings. As you pat the energy down to her feet, you are also helping her body to settle down and relax.

Movement 4 opens up her ears so she can listen.

Movements 5, 6, and 7 all work on opening the social senses. Movement 5 facilitates making eye contact and smiling. Movement 6 helps your child's tongue and lips form speech. Movement 7 helps him to be able to calm himself down when he is upset.

With Movements 8 and 9, you are strengthening digestion and helping your child eliminate toxins. Children with autism have a harder time getting rid of the chemicals that we encounter in daily life that can trigger difficult behavior. Over time, these can build up in their systems. Sometimes, you may get a strange taste in your mouth when you do the massage, and your child may pass a dark green, smelly bowel movement afterwards. These are immediate indicators of success. Your child is starting to clean out.

With Movements 10 and 11, you are helping to move energy all the way down into the legs and feet. Once it fills the toes, it circulates back up to the lower belly to restore physical vitality. Finally, Movement 12 sends the energy all the way up to the head to nourish the brain.

After a couple of months, your child may reach for your hand and place it on her forehead, chest, or belly. This signals that the deep energy fields are open and ready to fill up. This is wonderful! Just rest your hand gently on the area, stay longer on it, relax, and enjoy the connection.

Do I need to do the movements in order and all at once?

Ideally, the movements are done in order in one session, but at first, it can be hard to accomplish this. Touch can be so difficult for a child who has autism that the whole massage is too much for him to accept at one time. That's okay. Start with the first movement and see how far you go. Do part of it, and then pick up where you left off and finish up later. In other words, do the movements in order, but you don't have to do them all at once. Within a week or two it should become easier for both of you to do the whole thing in one session.

The important thing to understand about this massage, and about Chinese medicine in general, is that treatments in response to individual symptoms are never just about the individual symptoms. Chinese medicine always looks at the body as a whole. Western medicine likes to take a one-symptom-one-treatment approach, but because everything is connected in the body and what happens in one area influences the rest (as the health of the whole also affects the performance of the parts), the Chinese treatment looks at a unified picture. All of this is to say that it takes all of the pieces to make the massage work. Each of the pieces has effects, but taken as a whole, the massage has general effects throughout the body. Yes, it might be hard to get the whole massage done at first, but that must be the ultimate goal, and most families find they can accomplish the whole massage in one session within a matter of days.

Can I use the movements outside of the massage time?

The single most important thing is that you do the entire massage, in order, at least once a day. Of course you can do it twice a day—families who do it twice a day see faster progress in their child—but once a day is perfectly adequate. You can also do extra of some movements during the day. As you'll see at the end of the discussion on the movements, there are some movements that are especially helpful for certain things.

How am I going to get my child to lie still for a massage?

In short, you aren't. This is a process, and children can be very wriggly. You will have to be persistent, especially at the beginning. It makes things easier to have a partner helping you so one person can either hold or stabilize your child while the other does the massage. Initially, you might feel like you are working hard to get the whole massage in during the day, sneaking in a few movements now and then as you see the opportunity. It's okay. As the channels open, your child will be able to settle down more for the massage. Try to create the idea of a certain place and time for the massage from the start, even if it doesn't turn out that way for a while.

Is it okay to distract my child with a toy or DVD?

Absolutely. The energy benefits will happen for your child whether he is paying attention or not, and a DVD can make the massage a lot easier in the beginning.

Over time, the distractions will no longer be necessary because the child is enjoying the close connection time with his parent.

Every time you do the massage for your child, you are building toward future success. You might not see improvement in one day, but it is cumulative. Without the difficult first days, you won't get to the easier days a few weeks down the road.

Are two adults giving the massage better than one?

There is no doubt that two parents make it easier, especially at the beginning, but one parent can definitely give the massage alone. You know more than anyone how to read your child and work with him. When he squirms, put him back in position and keep going. Do this gently and matter-of-factly and consider it part of the massage; you have to stay calm. Having the second parent can be helpful—in fact, there are some specific supporting postures for the second parent covered at the end of the 12 movements—but don't let the unavailability of a second parent prevent the massage. Go for it!

What if parts of the massage seem to hurt?

This is a tricky issue. Your child is more attuned to your touch and voice than anybody else's. You are the person most likely to touch her in the way that will seem most natural to her. You are going to encounter places that are very uncomfortable to the touch—those being the places that are causing your child the most problems and are going to ultimately need the most help; the ears, fingers, and toes are common. We never, ever, want to cause harm to a child with our touch, so it is always gentle. Even after several months of massage, the pressure never exceeds that with which we would give a big hug to a small child, but in the beginning, your child will react in some places as if you are hurting him. It is important that you note those areas and study this book to learn how to best address them. As a general rule, though, only you can judge what is too much based on your child's reactions. At first, the discomfort might be too overwhelming for the child to tolerate and you might have to take a break between massage movements. That said, you have to find a balance. Your child can tolerate some discomfort—after all, she is already uncomfortable, and you have to find a way to work through that discomfort a bit at a time. Just remember that everything you are able to accomplish will get you closer to the time when the massage becomes easier and routine.

Should I force my child to have the massage?

No! If you force a child who is actively kicking, hitting, angry, or fearful, into submitting to a 15-minute ordeal, his nervous system will be in full "fight or flight" mode, and will most likely be stuck there for some time. It won't be helpful to trigger this and, in fact, it will be counterproductive.

This is where a professional trainer can be helpful, but without one, you as a parent can still figure out ways to work through this. It takes some grit and persistence on your part, but if you don't do it, your child won't get the benefit of the massage. Perhaps you can try again later, and do a small piece of it at a time. Perhaps you will initially use a partner who can distract the child and help keep him in position while you go through the movements. It will get easier. The really difficult times usually last only a week or two, at most a month. You have to have faith that no matter how imperfect the early attempts might be, they are creating the conditions that will make it easier down the road.

If you don't start somewhere and keep going, you won't get to the destination. The first weeks can be trying, but whatever you accomplish in those early days will help.

Does my child always have to be lying down for the movements? Could one parent hold him on her lap for some of the movements?

At first, you may not be able to get your child to lie down for the movements. You may even have to chase him around the room to do the massage. It is always helpful if one parent gently corrals the child in her arms and on her lap while the other works on the child. But as you persist, one of the goals is for the child to lie down on his own for the massage. If he won't lie down on his belly, it means that he has a block in his energy flow somewhere that needs your help. Once you've addressed it, he will lie down easily.

There are some movements that are particularly uncomfortable for my child. Is it okay if I skip those?

Qigong massage is a treatment and, as we know, sometimes treatments that ultimately help us are not comfortable. Discomfort at gentle touch carries with it important information for us. It is showing us where the biggest problems lie. And so, contrary to our instinct to avoid an area, discomfort is an indicator that we must spend extra time there. The strategy is to adjust the touch, make it lighter and quicker, or slower and pressing, depending on what the child accepts best, and spend more time in problem areas, doing the movements additional times. Over time, the discomfort will be replaced with pleasure and relaxation.

Discomfort with gentle touch is a signal that your child needs extra help there. Figure out whether the area is blocked or empty, and you will know how to adjust your touch.

Is more better in general?

The research shows that once a day for five months works. You don't have to do more than that. Some people like to do the massage twice a day as a nice way to begin the day and to end it, for example, and the children tend to progress faster that way. But again, the research shows that once a day for five months is enough.

What about self-care for parents who give qigong massage?

On occasion, parents have reported feeling slightly sick or head-achy after giving the massage, as if they have picked up some of their child's toxins. You can help to clear this by washing your hands and taking a walk outside.

Our bodies continuously clear the toxins we encounter in daily life, and we can flush them out immediately with a qigong exercise routine. There is a 15-minute exercise routine called *Self-Care Qigong* available on our website that you can do at home. These exercises naturally clear out toxins and fill you with energy, leaving you calmer and more relaxed for the day. You can do your qigong exercise routine after the massage or at any time of day. It is a good addition to your self-care.

Many of our parents do qigong exercise routines in their homes or take qigong classes in the community where they can practice with a group and receive feedback. We recommend that you make a qigong exercise routine part of your daily life.

Chapter 4

THE MASSAGE

Before you begin to do qigong massage with your child, read this chapter and watch the videos located at www.jkp.com/voucher using the code QIGONGMASSAGE. Then practice the 12 movements with a partner until you feel you can do them calmly and smoothly. This practice is very important. While it is tempting to jump right in with your child, resist! Once you are comfortable with the information in this chapter and can do the 12 movements smoothly with the help of the Movement Chart (see page 141–142), you are ready to start with your child.

Once you've begun, you will have questions, and there are some more concepts for you to understand in order to get the most out of the massage. Be sure to visit the material in Chapters 5 and 6. You might not remember it all after one reading, but, after you've revisited it a few times in the early weeks of the treatment and you've had some experience with the techniques, it will all fall into place.

You need to be as calm and confident with the motions as possible when you begin with your child so you can fully engage in what is happening with him. If you are distracted and trying to learn the movements while at the same time dealing with your child's reactions to the massage, it increases the chances that you will get off to a rough start. Why make it harder on yourself? Find somebody to work through the movements with. Additionally, there is some more helpful information to know once you have mastered the 12 basic movements.

More than going through the motions–but that's a start!

You will find that as the months pass, your understanding of how to best do the massage for your child will grow. You will know that on any given day, you will need to adjust to how she is responding to your touch. You will recognize when you've encountered a trouble spot and you will know how to deal with it. And, best of all, your child will become increasingly more receptive to the massage as her channels open. Over time, she might start to ask you to adjust the massage, pressing harder, going faster and lighter, spending more time on an area, or just pressing your hand against an area of her body to help it fill with energy and blood.

There is a troubleshooting guide in Chapter 6. It is good to read it often to remind yourself of what it contains so you can reference it as things come up during the massage.

Don't worry about knowing everything all at once, or even at being good at the massage at the start. Like anything worth knowing how to do, it takes some practice. You'll get better and, as we said, if you follow the instructions, even if you aren't perfect, you won't harm your child. When you've finished the book, watched the videos, and practiced, you will remember some things, but not everything. Don't sweat it beyond that. Use the Movement Chart as a guide until you know the movements automatically and come back to the materials often to check your understanding and to pick up more skills so you can continue to improve the effectiveness of your massage. Beyond that, it's all on the upside, so take the plunge!

Form, awareness, intention: Important elements for success

In addition to learning the movements, the person giving the massage must think about and practice three important elements of the treatment: Form, Awareness, and Intention.

Form

Another word for form is technique. Your form alone determines 30 percent of what is possible with this treatment. Are your hands starting and ending in the right places? Are you carefully following the channels as shown on the Movement Chart? Are you spending the appropriate amount of time with each movement, or are you rushing through the massage? Is your child in a comfortable place and are you able to perform the massage easily in the space you are using?

A smooth and continuous execution of the movements is not the end goal; tuning in to your child so you can clear blocks and fill emptiness is.

Awareness

Think about how good it feels to really connect with someone, to have a sense of being seen and heard. It feels like there is a lot of communication going on, whether verbal or non-verbal, because you are on the same wavelength. The massage makes communication happen between your hands and your child's body. If you are watching his face, his hands, and his body, and paying attention to how he tenses or relaxes as you massage—and then you respond to that—there is an energy flow happening between the two of you. It is like a direct body communication that says, "I feel you, and when you show me something, I respond to you."

For example, you might be tapping your child's neck during the massage. You notice that he starts to turn his head so a different part of his neck is under your fingers. Instead of moving on past the area, you continue to tap. He keeps turning his head to move a different area under your fingers. It's like a cat saying "scratch here, scratch here." After a few minutes, he stops and you go on to the next part of the massage. He showed you what he needed, and you responded.

It's like surfing together; as the wave moves, you move with it, gently rebalancing on the board all the while. It is all about finding the right touch at the right moment for the right part of your child's body. This might sound a little overwhelming, but realize that you have already been doing this for your child's entire life. When you found the best way to burp him or how to move his sleeping body from car to bed, you were adjusting your touch to his response in the way you knew to be best.

Intention

The parent's ability to focus and hold an intention can account for a whopping 70 percent of the effectiveness of the massage. This is one reason why it is important to be physically and *mentally* ready to give the massage before you start.

The word "intention" has a special meaning in the practice of qigong. It has to do with the ability to keep the goal for each movement in mind as you do it. For example, if you are doing a movement for which the goal is to get the qi flowing down from the head clear to the feet, there is a lot of body to traverse before you get there, and you are likely to run into some problem spots along the way! If you keep the *movement goal* in mind—the intention—you will adjust to your child's responses more appropriately and ultimately achieve success.

A second part of the intention piece is the goal that you want your child to eagerly enter the world and more fully connect with it and you. As you go through the massage, you will be creating openings through which the child can begin to see and experience the world more accurately. Part of intention is creating a welcoming, safe place that your child will want to emerge into. If you keep a cheerful, connecting, warm intention as you give the massage, it will help your child immeasurably as his senses begin to open. Make it light, be cheerful, be calm and matter-of-fact in dealing with the rough spots. Initially, you might need to be reassuring: "You're okay." Later, you might name the body parts as you pat them, helping with language acquisition. The specifics of what you say are up to you, but always, always, be there in the moment, smiling, chatting, singing. When she becomes able, your child will join you there.

Before you begin each day's massage

Before you begin the massage each day, it is important to prepare yourself physically and emotionally to give this time to your child. Make it part of your practice to do the following steps as preparation.

- Be sure there is good air flow in the room.

- Assess yourself physically to be sure you have enough energy to give the massage.

- Assess yourself emotionally to be sure you can perform the massage with loving intention. Let go of all your other cares and thoughts for the time being. Prepare to be emotionally present for this time with your child.

- Prepare your hands to give the massage.

- Watch the accompanying videos to see a demonstration of how to do the first two steps in the following list:

  ○ Stand straight, but relaxed, arms to the side. Turn your palms up and, bending only at the elbow, raise your hands in front of you to waist level and then lower them back to your sides. Do this three times, feeling the air move against your arms and hands, letting go of everything else in your day and getting ready to be with your child.

  ○ Elbows at your side, hold your hands in front of you at waist level. Cupping your hands, bring them toward one another slowly until you feel the warmth of the other hand like a soft ball between your hands, and then slowly take them back to a neutral position—roughly shoulder width. Breathe gently and fully as you do this motion.

o   Alternatively, you can rub your hands together however it feels best. Do this three times to prepare your loving energy to flow to your child.

Why do I need to assess my physical state before I begin?

Giving qigong massage gives some of your energy to your child. Although the massage generally leaves you and the child both feeling better, if your own energy is particularly depleted by exhaustion, stress, or illness on a certain day, you need to consider if you have appropriate reserves for yourself before you begin. There are times when we simply don't have any extra energy to give to someone else. Those are times *not* to give the massage. When the barrel is empty, there is no water for anyone.

Why do I need to be emotionally calm before I give the massage?

Our emotions have very strong energy–both positive and negative–and parents and children can readily feel each other's emotions. Energy doesn't lie; if you are agitated while giving the massage, it is much more difficult to find that loving parent place within you to connect with your child, and your child is much more likely to pick up your agitation. Just as much as positive emotions contribute to healing, negative emotions contribute to stress and illness. One of the reasons parent-provided qigong massage is so effective is because of the profound love and commitment a parent feels for her child, love beyond all reason. When a parent is relaxed, and focuses on his child to give her massage, this calm loving energy is what is transmitted through touch and voice. The massage movements are designed to make the most of that transfer of calm, loving energy.

General instructions

Repetitions

The instructions for each movement show a minimum number of times you should do each one *but you can do more*. As you become more skilled, you will find yourself repeating the movements many more times or spending more time in one place or another depending on how your child is responding and what she needs that day. Typically, the whole set might take 10–15 minutes, but it could take twice that long.

Touch

This qigong massage is actually about patting and pressing, more than it is rubbing or kneading muscle as we typically think of massage. Watching the videos will give you a good sense of how to do the pats, but practicing with someone other than your child will help you best understand how to use the appropriate weight and speed. There needs to be some weight in your pats to move the energy under the skin, similar to the weight of hand you might use to burp a baby. It must be firm and intentional—you want that gas bubble to rise, that qi to move—but it is never hard or hurtful. Most people give the massage from the side, but position yourself where you feel most comfortable. Except for around the ears, it doesn't matter in what direction your hands are pointing. It's the direction of the patting and the touch that matter.

Your child will tell you with words or body language to move faster or slower, heavier or lighter, and you will learn to automatically "tune" your touch to your child. Remember, though, that unlike most other times you touch your child during the day, there is an end result you are working toward. If, for example, you find an area on your child's head, hands, or feet that is uncomfortable, don't avoid it. That's a place where your child needs some extra help. Try a lighter pat, going a bit quicker, and making a few extra passes over the area. If your child is ticklish, in a spot, it is empty. Gently press there instead of patting. If the fingers or toes are uncomfortable, press them gently instead of rubbing them. Listen, watch, and adjust.

Shape of your massage hand

The shape of your hand is important in the massage for two reasons: it ensures a more comfortable touch, and it better transmits your energy. If you think about your palm and how you use it to interact with people, you'll realize that is a point of *connection* with other people. We greet people by pressing palms in a handshake. We shake hands to show respect; we hold hands to communicate love.

There is a hollow at the center of the palm from which qi-energy connects directly to the heart. If you begin to watch for it, you'll see that humans instinctively use this connecting point—it is like a conduit into our emotional core. We even show it to others as we wave in greeting or goodbye. We talk about "loving touch" coming from the hands in Western thought. In Chinese medicine terms, we are transmitting qi-energy from our heart through our palm. When we cup our hands slightly, we create a little air space in the palm. It is filled with qi-energy. And so we pat with a slightly cupped hand. From a practical point of view, you need to cup your hand slightly so you aren't using a flat hand on your child, but at the same time keep your fingers relaxed enough to mold to your child's body. You can see how this works when you watch the videos.

When you work on the ears, it is a little different. You are cupping *around* the back of the ears, but not actually patting the ears with your palm. That would hurt. Also, be careful to spread your fingers, so that air passes between them. You don't want to be pushing air into the ear itself. This cupped hand, with the fingers slightly spread, causes your fingers to naturally land on the points behind that ear that will help to open it.

Don't forget to remove headgear and hair clasps or ties from your child's head before you start. Earrings, bracelets, and necklaces are fine as long as they don't get in your way.

Intention

In the description for each movement that follows, we've included a stated intention, or goal, for the movement. Think about teaching a child to ride a bike. As a parent, you have an intention that she will learn to ride it, but you know it will take a while. You will be right there to guide her, but, in the end, she is going to learn to ride at her own pace. Working with your child's energy is the same; you can't force it with your will, but you can guide it with your hands and knowledge, and support your child emotionally while she goes through the bumps of learning something new. You have to decide when you've made enough progress for the day on a particular step, and some days you'll feel like you're making more progress than others. Everything you do will help, so use your parents' wisdom and knowledge of your own child to know when it's time to move on.

Responses

There are a number of responses that have specific meanings. We've included many of these within the descriptions of the movements, but we've also listed them in alphabetical order in the next chapter. It is very important that you become familiar with these responses and learn how to adapt the massage to them. For example, humming is a specific response that you might not notice unless you are attuned to it. The legs lifting, ticklishness, your child's hands resting on yours—paying attention and adapting to these responses is part of the Awareness piece (Form, Awareness, Intention) that is integral to your success.

Once you have the 12 movements of the massage under your belt, watching for your child's responses and understanding them will become one of the most fascinating and rewarding parts of the experience.

The movements

As you do these 12 qigong massage movements, keep in mind that each movement has intention—to open up blocks in the energy channels, to fill areas where the energy flow is weak and there isn't enough blood circulation, and to get the qi-energy moving through the body so your child can grow in a healthy and balanced way.

At first, nearly every place you work, except for the hands and feet, will have blocks that need to clear down and out. We use a fast light patting to help blocks clear. Watch your child's head and feet. Often he won't lie down to start with—or he keeps his head up. Your first goal is to get the energy flowing down from the head. Just do your work and watch his head—when he puts it down, you will know the energy is moving down. Once his energy is flowing down freely, it will fill in the circulation to his feet and you will notice that his feet are lying flat on the table.

As is demonstrated in the videos, when a block is releasing, the child will often join in the qigong and hum. When you hear the hum, just stay patting on that part, in the same way, until he stops humming, and then continue on down. After a block has cleared, the circulation can start filling in.

Movement 1

Opens the brain and senses.

Calms.

Counteracts walking on tiptoe.

Boosts the immune system.

Grounds the child's energy.

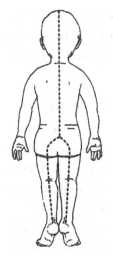

Do at least three times.

The starting point for Movement 1 is one of the two most important points that we use for the brain. It is begins right over what was the soft spot on top of the head. It is very important that you start at the right spot; if you miss it, the massage will be less effective. The illustration on the right shows the starting point.

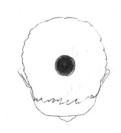

In the midline, where the skull bone and neck meet, is the second point that helps open up the brain. This point particularly helps the part of the brain that helps your child turn his face and make eye contact with you.

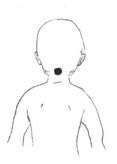

Child position: Lying on the belly, face down or turned to the side. If the child resists lying on his belly you can start with sitting or standing, but as soon as there is movement toward the floor, help him down.

Intention: To offer physical and emotional support while your child adapts to these first uncomfortable experiences of the massage. The energetic goal of the movement is to open the points to the brain and get the energy flowing toward the feet. The behavior you want to achieve is that your child can lie flat and relax for the massage.

The movement: With one hand, pat the soft spot on the top of the head until the neck relaxes and the child puts his head down. Then pat down the center of the back of the head, turning your hand sideways to pat at the base of the head until it relaxes. This patting at the back of the head is the second most important part of the massage. Continue to pat the energy down the neck and spine. When you reach the tailbone, pat down the middle of each leg to the outer ankles and end with several pats at the heels.

Watch for: Initially your child might not relax her neck and put her head down. In this case, pat the top of the head for a minute or so and then move on.

There is usually a block at the base of the skull and your child can get very wriggly when you pat here. If this happens, stay and pat gently where the skull meets the neck for a while until she starts to relax. Then move the energy on down the back and legs.

If your child's knees bend and the heels float up, do a few extra patting movements from the knees down to the feet. This will help the legs relax and lie flat.

Listen for: Humming. If your child begins to hum, stay at the spot that initiated it and pat until it stops.

Energy and circulation: When the points at the top of the head and where the skull meets the neck open up, the energy and blood flow improves and the brain can pay attention and learn. As pressure in the head is released down the back, head-banging stops. As energy flows naturally down the back to the heels, toe-walking stops. As the child is better able to ground his energy, it does not fly upwards when he is excited, and hand-flapping stops.

Over time: It can take a month or two for your child to be able to lie flat for the massage, relaxing his neck enough for him to put his head down and to allow you to pat his neck while remaining relaxed. Eventually, the legs will stay down and relaxed as well.

Signs of progress: Your child becomes aware of the world around him.

Movement 2

Restores normal sensation to the skin.

Can promote potty training.

Helps to clear toxins from the organs.

Promotes organ health and function.

Do at least three times.

Child position: Lying on the belly, face down or turned to the side.

Intention: To continue to provide physical and emotional support, while more points to the brain and organs open and more energy flows to the feet. Ultimately, your goal is to clear all the blocks that prevent your child from lying flat and quietly while you do this movement.

The movement: With a hand on either side of the soft spot on the top of the head, pat the top of the head a few times. Then, keeping the hands parallel, pat the energy down the back of the head. Turn one hand sideways to pat the neck, then use both hands, parallel again, to pat down either side of the spine and lower back, clear down the middle of the backs of the legs to the outer ankles and heels. End with a few extra pats on the heels.

Watch for: As with Movement 1, stay longer on the top of the head and neck if your child is wriggly. If your child's knees bend and the heels lift up, do a few extra patting movements from the knees down to the feet. If you notice that the child relaxes more with each pass, do this movement a few more times. If your child hums at some point as you progress down the body—a good sign!—stay at that point and continue patting until the humming stops.

  If you notice an unusual taste in your mouth or an unusual smell while you are doing this movement, it is because toxins are being released from your child's inner organs. Do some extra repetitions. This is generally true for any of the movements, but particularly for this one.

Listen for: Humming. Stay on the part that triggered the hum until it stops. If you are patting on the head, the head is opening up; over the chest, it means the lungs are opening up; over the lower back, the organs of the belly are releasing.

Energy and circulation: As the important points on the head and neck open up, the channels connecting the head and body open and flow freely. Blood circulation opens up to the whole back of the body, and normal feelings of pain and pleasure return to the skin. The child can feel when her diaper is wet or dirty, and when her bladder or bowel is full; potty training is easier. Under-sensitivity or over-sensitivity to touch balances out. As points on either side of the spine open up, they clear toxins from the organs beneath them, blood flow is improved, and the organs function better. The extra pats at the heels as you do the movement help to hold the energy down so it doesn't rush back up to the head.

Over time: The child stops wriggling and lies quietly. He begins to hum as you pat the areas where blocks are releasing. Later, when there are no more big blocks, your child will lie quietly on his stomach for the whole movement. His heels stay down because the circulation to the back of his body has filled in completely.

Signs of progress: If the child has not been crying when he is injured, expect this to change. If she has been unaware of her wet diaper, she will start to notice it.

Movement 3

Smoothes out emotions.

Increases tolerance for frustration.

Clears toxins from the body.

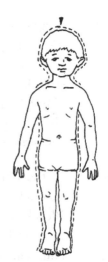

Do at least three times.

If your child gets angry easily and hits, kicks, or bites, this movement can be difficult at first. After a few weeks, it is usually easier and aggressive behavior decreases.

Child position: Lying on the back, face up.

Intention: To tune in to your child's responses and adjust to them. To ultimately clear all the blocks you encounter as you go down the sides.

The movement: This movement starts at the top of the head and comes down the sides. When you reach the ears, cup your hands loosely around them, fingers toward the back of the head, and spend extra time tapping there to help with the important points around the ears that are often blocked. Your fingers should have a little space between them; don't make a tight cup with your hand. Your child won't like the attention to his ears if they are blocked, but as long as you feel you aren't hurting him (you aren't boxing his ears or hitting them with a flat palm), persist. This is an important point in the massage. Pat down the sides of the neck, the tops of the shoulders, and then down the sides of the torso, the hips, legs, and on down to the ankles.

Watch for: Any kind of alternating or side-to-side movement of the head, arms, trunk, or legs. This indicates that the channels down the side of the body are activating and the qigong is working. Take note of blocks you encountered over the ears and side of the neck so you can spend more time on them again in Movement 4.

Energy and circulation:	The patting at the top of the head and the ear opens up the circulation to the ears and helps make the connection between the eyes and the ears so that the child can look and listen at the same time. As the sides of the body can work together, the child is better able to regulate his temper and emotions.
Over time:	When all the blocks to downward flow have been cleared, the child lies quietly. She may go through a period when she is ticklish, and you will adjust your touch to be slower with more pressure to help the circulation fill in completely.
Signs of progress:	Don't be surprised if your child stops looking out of the sides of his eyes. The incidence of aggression will drop dramatically.

Movement 4

Opens the ears and helps the child to listen.
Boosts language acquisition.

Do at least three times.

Child position: Lying on the back, face up.

Intention: To discover and clear blocks in the your child's ears and neck. To be ready to switch to the filling technique when the child's body language (e.g. ticklishness or her hand comes in to join yours) says it is time.

The movement: This movement begins with the hands forming a gentle cup over the ears, with fingers in the back of the ears. Pat behind the ear and then move down the side of the neck, watching for tension in the neck to release, spending extra time on the neck if you need to, and then move across the top of the shoulder and down the arm to the back of the hand. It's nice to pat with one hand and hold your child's hand with the other while you do this.

Watch for: Discomfort around the ear and side of the neck, especially if your child has had a lot of ear infections or if she doesn't seem to notice your voice and hasn't started talking yet. If it is uncomfortable for your child, it is especially important to do extra repetitions of this movement. Go lighter and quicker over the area, but do it.

If the ears or neck are ticklish instead of uncomfortable, use a slow, gentle, pulsing pressure around the ear instead of tapping. If your child's hand comes up and rests on yours, also switch to the slower, pressure technique demonstrated in the online materials.

If your child resists or pushes your hand away, you can try patting the ear and the top of the shoulder at the same time, or try patting down the arm several times starting just below the ear. Then try patting the ear again.

Listen for: "Ow"—this means you have to adjust your touch. Listen for the hum, and continue on that area in the same way until the hum stops.

Energy and   In autism, there are often layers of block around the ear. The child
circulation: will go through a time when she needs the quick light pats, followed by a time when she wants slow pressing movement. This reflects a layer of block clearing and then the circulation filling in. Then, the child will progress to the next deeper layer of block, and that will have to be cleared and filled in. This can happen many times until the circulation through the ear is full and free-flowing.

Over time: This area will start to feel better for your child and you won't have to be as careful around it.

Signs of progress: As your child becomes less resistant to touch around the ears, she starts to notice you speaking, and to understand what you are saying to her. Once she can pay attention and understand what is being said to her, she'll want to start expressing herself by talking.

So that you don't have to keep moving back and forth around your child, you can do Movements 4, 5, and 6 together on one side before moving to the other side to do them there.

Movement 5

Helps the child open up socially.
Facilitates eye contact and facing toward people.

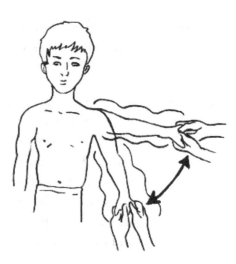

Do at least three times for each arm.

Child position: Lying on the back, face up.

Intention: To attract and keep your child's attention.

To connect. While doing this movement, you are using the shaking movement and your voice to attract your child's attention, to get your child to turn her face to yours, and to make eye contact. Once you have eye contact, your intention is to keep it as long as the child is comfortable by making the rest of the movement playful.

The movement: Standing at your child's side, look at her face, and hold her hand in both of yours. Grasp your child's hand between your thumb and forefinger, one hand grasping between the second and third fingers, the other hand between the third and fourth. The rest of your hand folds around your child's naturally and comfortably.

Pull gently on your child's arm until it is fully extended. You don't want the elbow to be bent. Be sure that her wrist is neutral, not bent, so the energy can flow straight down the arm and out the fingers. Gently shaking the arm, move it in an arc from the side to level with the shoulder and back. (Think of making angel wings in the snow, one arm at a time.) Do this with a gentle, playful attitude, looking at the child's face and saying, for example, "up, up, up" and "down, down, down" as you move the arm up and down.

Watch for: Your child turning to face you and make eye contact as you do this movement. If the shoulder is tense and lifts, do several quick patting movements from the side of the neck down and across the top of the shoulder to the arm to help relax it back down.

Energy and circulation: The movement sends a wave of energy into the chest to open the child's heart center, which the Chinese call the middle dantien. This is the center of feelings and of wanting to connect with other human beings.

Over time: Your child will make eye contact with you and smile as you do this movement. This means the movement is coordinating the basic brain reflexes needed for social interaction—the ability to face a person, make eye contact, tune the ear to the person's voice, and open to him or her. You might begin to chat together or sing little songs.

Signs of progress: Your child will make eye contact with you more often. Over time, he will start to make connections to other people, too.

Movement 6

Helps with speech.

Do at least three times for each hand.

Child position: Lying on the back, face up.

Intention: To clear any blocks related to each finger and to fill them with pressing motions when needed.

The movement: Holding your child's hand gently with one hand, use the forefinger and thumb of the other to gently rub the sides of each finger with short alternating strokes from the base to the fingertip. If the fingers are especially tender, press them gently instead of rubbing.

Watch for: Tender or ticklish fingers indicate that there is not enough circulation. Switch from rubbing to gently pressing. You might notice that one finger is more sensitive than others. Repeat the pressing movements until the fingers are not sensitive anymore.

Sometimes this movement triggers big movements of the legs. Repeat the movement until the legs stop moving. This is a sign that the child is making brain connections between the hands and feet.

It is common for a child who is not yet talking to move his tongue and lips during this movement. This is a positive sign, because it indicates that the brain is forming the connections necessary for speech. You should continue rubbing until this movement stops.

Listen for: There will be a time when the chest is first opening that your child may start giggling and laughing delightedly. This means the feeling center is opening up and he is experiencing joy.

Energy and circulation: At first there is usually not enough circulation in the fingers, and they are uncomfortable. Later, once the blood flow has been reestablished, the fingers will be comfortable and relaxed. Each finger is connected to a different part of the body: the thumb to the lungs, the index to the sinuses, the third finger to the heart, the ring finger to the ears, and the fifth finger to the tongue for the formation of speech.

Over time: The sensitive areas will ease and your child will enjoy the finger massage.

Signs of progress: Speech improves.

Movement 7

Helps with self-soothing.

Helps with transitions.

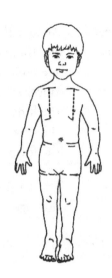

Do at least three times.

Child position: Lying on the back, face up.

Intention: To trigger and reinforce the self-soothing mechanisms in the autonomic nervous system. Rubbing the eyes and yawning are indications that this is happening.

The movement: Using both hands, slowly and gently press the chest from the collarbone, down along the nipple line to the bottom of the ribcage. Remember, the ribs are made to move in and out as we breathe, so this doesn't hurt. Use enough pressure to move the ribs, about what you might use when hugging your child. Repeat the movements until your child rubs her eyes and yawns.

Watch for: Signs of sleepiness, such as rubbing the eyes and yawning, indicate that the self-soothing mechanisms are being triggered. Once this has happened, do more repetitions to reinforce the response in the nervous system.

Especially watch for her hands moving up near yours or even on them. This means the chest is open and filling with calming energy. If this happens, put your hands over hers and continue for longer, taking her hands through the movement with you.

Listen for: Initially your child might hum or sing with this movement. Later he will rest quietly.

Energy and circulation: Deep in the chest is the middle dantien, the energy source for our feeling, social self. As this opens up, the child expresses his feelings more. "I feel sad, Mommy," "I feel happy, Daddy."

Once this area opens, it will naturally start to fill with energy, both from the child and from the parents. See support hands on page 69 for instructions on how you can help this filling happen.

Over time: Your child will become calm and rub his eyes and yawn more quickly when you start this movement.

Signs of progress: Transitions become easier and the child can self-soothe.

After a few months of massage, your child can become very relaxed during the massage. If this happens, and both parents are available, consider adding support hands to the massage. This technique is described on page 69.

Movement 8

Helps with digestion.

Helps with diarrhea or constipation.

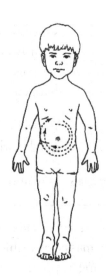

Do three sets of nine.

Child position: Lying on the back, face up.

Intention: To clear and strengthen the digestive system. To watch for blocks and be prepared to move them down the legs. To watch for emotions, and be prepared to allow the space for them to bubble up and release. To know when it is time to add parent support hands and be prepared to add them.

The movement: This movement consists of gently moving your hand in large circles around the belly button. The direction (clockwise or counterclockwise) you rub—or "stir"—is very important. There are three sets of nine circles. You start in one direction, reverse direction for nine circles, and then return to the original direction. If your child's bowel movements are loose or normal, stir nine circles clockwise, nine counterclockwise, then nine clockwise. If she is constipated, begin with counterclockwise motion, stirring nine times, then reverse to clockwise for nine times, and return to counterclockwise. The counterclockwise motion is always lighter and faster than the clockwise. When you stir counterclockwise, think of drawing a spiral of blocked energy up and out. When you stir clockwise, slow way down and think of sending your energy inward. This sounds complicated, but is actually easy to remember. Think of loosening a screw or a faucet – turning counterclockwise – to get poop out. Or, think of tightening it by turning clockwise if you need to tighten it up. If the poop is normal, we "normally" think of turning a screw to the right, which is clockwise.

Watch for: If your child becomes very relaxed and begins to hum deep in her chest, the energy source in her lower belly is filling. Slow down and do some extra clockwise motion until the humming stops. If the knees draw up gently, it is an indication that the belly is filling. Continue the clockwise motion until they relax back down.

If the knees draw up tightly, there is an energy blockage that is having trouble clearing down the legs. Interrupt the rubbing of the belly to pat down the tops of the legs from the thighs down, using a quick patting motion until the legs relax. Then resume where you left off. Keep doing the clockwise and counterclockwise movements until the legs are relaxed. If your child's hands come up onto yours, it means the lower belly energy source is starting to fill. Slow down and continue.

Listen for: A low, deep humming. This means the energy of the lower belly is filling in and strengthening. Continue what you are doing until the humming stops.

Energy and circulation: This movement helps the bowels clear out constipation or ends diarrhea and strengthens the ability to absorb nourishment. Deep in the belly is the lower dantien, the center for physical vitality. Once the bowels are functioning normally, this center can begin to fill. You can help it to fill by using support hands (see page 69).

Over time: You will need to change the order of "stirring" as your child's bowel movements begin to change.

Signs of progress: Your child's bowels will begin to function more normally. Constipation or diarrhea will abate and your child's appetite will improve. She will start eating more and trying new foods, and her physical health will improve.

We help to clear a block with a fast light motion counterclockwise (like taking out a screw or turning on a faucet.) We turn energy in with slow pressing clockwise motions (fastening the screw or turning the faucet off).

Movement 9

Helps clear toxins from the belly.
Strengthens the legs.

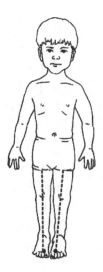

Do at least three times

Movement 9 is very important because it opens up the channels that drain toxins from the belly area.

Child position: Lying on the back, face up.

Intention: To clear the blocks in the legs and fill them, and to make sure that the connection between the belly and legs is strong and open.

The movement: Using a hand for each leg, pat from the tops of the thighs, down to the shins and on down to the tops of the feet.

Watch for: If your child draws his knees up during this motion, it means that his body is trying to clear things out. Continue patting lightly and quickly on the upper thighs until the legs start to relax downward.

    If the legs are ticklish or sensitive, there is not enough blood circulation. Instead of light quick pats, apply more pressure and slow down.

Listen for: Giggling or "ow"—indicating the legs are empty, and you need to switch to slow pressure.

Energy and circulation: First the blood flow is reaching the skin, and then it is filling into the legs. If the legs were weak, they will become stronger.

Over time: Your child will relax and enjoy the patting.

Signs of progress: After the first few massages, your child may pass one or more dark green, sticky, smelly bowel movements. This is a great thing because it means he is clearing out old bile from his liver. If he was constipated, his bowel movements will become more normal. Leg strength can improve.

By the time you reach Movement 10, you and the child should have both relaxed to the point where you complete the last three steps almost in silence.

Movement 10

Calms.

Helps with sleep.

Do about nine times.

Child position: Lying on the back, face up.

Intention: To bring all the qi down to the legs and heels, which will allow the child to calm down and relax.

The movement: Using both hands, one leg at a time, use slow, even strokes starting behind the knees and ending with the heel. Alternate hands, one hand starting behind the knee as the other is ending at the heel. Continue until your child's leg is loose and relaxed.

Watch for: If your child is ticklish or giggly when you do this, it means the area is weak or empty. Go even slower and apply more pressure or switch to gently squeezing your way down the calf.

Listen for: By now you and your child should be silent.

Energy and circulation: These long sweeping movements bring the energy and circulation down to the heels and feet, thus grounding the child, and settling him down.

Over time: If you are doing the massage before bedtime, your child will be falling asleep by the time you get to this movement.

Signs of progress: Sleep and bedtime become easier.

Movement 11

Clears the legs and belly.
Fills in the toes.

Do up to three times for each toe.

Child position: Lying on the back, face up.

Intention: To fill the energy into the toes and be ready to rub, press, or "bicycle" as needed.

The movement: As you did with Movement 6 on the hands, use your forefinger and thumb to gently rub the sides of each toe from the base to the nail. It's hard to do this with tiny toes, so if you can't get to the base, rub along the sides as best you can. Always remember to go in the direction of base to nail. If the toes are too sensitive, gently press the top and bottom of each toe gently.

The bicycle adaptation of Movement 11: If your child pulls back his foot because even the pressing is too uncomfortable, "go with" the movement, and guide his foot into a motion as if he were peddling a bicycle. This uses the big muscles of the leg to send down the blood to the toes. Each time the foot comes down, you press the blood into a toe. Holding that toe, you do another cycle of the bicycle, and as the foot comes down again, you move to pressing the next toe. Continue until you have done all the toes.

Watch for: If one toe is more sensitive than the others, press it gently instead of rubbing it, but spend a little extra time on it.

Listen for: An "ow" or giggling, indicating that there is not enough circulation in the toes. If you hear this, immediately switch to pressing gently. Do not move the skin on the sides of the toes, just press.

Energy and circulation: At first there is almost never enough circulation in the toes. It is very common to need to use the bicycle motion. This uses the big muscles of the leg to send blood down to the toes to help fill them. Each toe is connected to a different part of the body: the big toe, second, and third to digestion, the fourth to the liver and gallbladder, and the fifth to the kidney and bladder.

Over time: Later on, if you began with the bicycle motion, you can switch to pressing, and then even later move on to rubbing the toes without your child drawing her feet away. The toes will progressively become less sensitive and your child will enjoy this part of the massage.

Signs of progress: Cutting the toenails will become easier, motor skills will improve, and general health will improve.

Movement 12

Sends energy to the brain.

Helps to fill the three dantien to promote physical vitality, sociability, and learning.

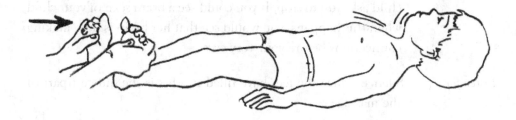

Do one set of nine pulses. Can repeat several times.

Child position: Lying on the back, face up.

Intention: To have brought the child into a state of relaxation by this time in the massage. To send nourishing energy, with each pulse, from the feet to the head, nourishing the belly, the chest, and the brain.

The movement: Make sure that your child's head and body are aligned and straight. Sometimes you will need a partner to gently hold the head in a neutral position to keep the neck from turning to the side. Take a foot in each hand with the thumb and forefinger positioned as shown below. If the feet are too sensitive initially, place your palms against the soles and let your fingers curve over the top. You eventually want to move toward pressing with your fingers in the proper place, but you might have to work into that.

Brace yourself with one foot ahead of the other and your back straight. Gently press against the feet nine times in a slow regular pulse. Because you are going slowly, it can help you to count out loud. Focus on sending your good energy into your child's system, filling up the empty spaces clear to the brain. After one set of nine, ask your child if she wants another set and repeat as many times as your child wants.

Watch for: You'll see the tip of the chin move slightly if you are doing this correctly. If you see small twitching movements happen in your child's face, keep repeating the movement until they stop or the child asks you to stop. If you could see a brain scan of your child when this happens, you would see that her brain is busy making connections before your very eyes.

Listen for: Silence. Once the feet have filled in, this is the quietest part of the massage.

Energy and circulation: The energy you brought down to the feet will transform to nourishing circulation: energy that you are sending back up through the body to fill in all the empty spaces and nourish the brain.

Over time: The feet are often the last places for circulation to fully fill in. It might take several months until the toes are not sensitive any more.

Signs of progress: You will see progress in learning and development.

Rest: The important last step
Enables the body to integrate

Once the massage is over, it is important to let the child lie quietly as long he likes. There have been a lot of subtle—and occasionally not-so-subtle—changes made to the child's energy flow during the course of the massage. He needs time to make the new connections you've created openings for, and for his body and emotions to adjust. When your child is ready, he will get up on his own or go off to sleep. Follow your child's lead. He might want to finish the massage with a hug before he gets up and transitions to another activity. Otherwise, sleep is good. The connections will continue to be made.

If your child is hyper after the massage, it means that the energy is not flowing freely down from the head yet. You have moved the energy during the massage, but it is flaring back up and bouncing back against the block(s) in the head, ears, or neck. This is important information, because it tells you that the next time you do the massage, you will want to spend more time on the first four movements. Also, until you get the energy down, you will want to do the massage earlier in the day.

Support hands
Performed by one parent while the other completes Movements 8-11

It is both nice and healthy for your child if both parents are able to participate in the massage. Over time, it becomes a relaxing, connected time for all who are involved. Once your child has learned to relax while you go through the movements, there is a wonderful opportunity to boost the massage benefits even further.

We've talked a bit about the three dantien located in the head, chest, and belly. One of the difficulties caused by autism is that these reservoirs become empty or weak. In Chinese medicine, this is referred to as deficiency and is one of the primary causes of disease. This weakness is manifested in your child by delays in development—cognitive, emotional, and physical. Because the parents' energy can flow from the palms into these area—once they are open and accepting—thanks to the effects of the massage, a parent can literally help to fill them with his or her hands. You will know when your child is ready for this because his body and face will be quiet and relaxed. The blocks that have prevented these areas from filling are gone and your child can absorb what you offer. Know that doing this will help your child fill up with good healing energy so he can better learn and grow.

Support hands can be offered by one parent when the other parent is doing Movements 8–11. Feel free to trade off on this.

The head area can be accessed with a gentle hand on the forehead, the chest by covering the heart, and the lower energy source with a hand just below the belly button.

Typically, children prefer the father's energy on chest and belly, because males tend to have a more energizing effect. Children tend to prefer the mother's connection to be on the head and chest. *Always go with your child's preference on this.* He will intuitively know what he needs.

Giving support hands is remarkably easy. Simply rest your hands gently on the area, relax, and feel your connection with your child. It doesn't add a long time to the massage and your child will let you know when they've had enough. Most parents report that both they and the child are energized by this exchange.

A few golden reminders

Always move down the body

Never do the movements *up* the body. You must always be moving the energy down toward the feet or fingers. Going in the wrong direction could give your child a headache and would not help his autism at all.

Do the whole massage at least once a day

Do not pick and choose between the movements. Do the whole thing, in the proper order. Autism affects many layers and systems of the body and the whole body needs support—not just the belly, for example. Plus, the success of each movement is dependent on the movement that preceded it and on the movement that follows it.

Discomfort means that your child needs extra help in that area

Our instinct, if our child expresses discomfort, is to stop what we're doing. Discomfort is an indication that you've found the kind of problem area the massage is intended to help. You have to find the right kind of touch to address the discomfort depending on the factors described in the movements and troubleshooting chapters (Chapters 5 and 6). You might need to tap quicker and lighter, do more repetitions, or go slower and use more pressure. Your child's reactions will determine the correct approach.

You are not limited to doing each movement three times

You can do extra repetitions of the movements as you are working through the areas if you feel your child needs and tolerates more attention with a particular movement.

Locked-up emotions can be expressed during the massage. Keep doing what you were doing

Don't be surprised if your child suddenly expresses a strong emotion during the massage. This usually happens a few months into the treatment and the emotion is typically sorrow. *Don't stop what you're doing!* This is an indication that the areas that have been holding these emotions are opening up and healing. It is a wonderful sign. Anticipate this so you are prepared if it happens. Your instinct will be to stop and comfort your child. It is hard to resist, but in this circumstance, you just need to keep going with the massage, repeating whatever movement you are doing until the emotion is completely released. Try to stay as matter-of-fact and calm as possible. Whatever space you had provided for this release to occur needs to be maintained so the emotion can come all the way out and your child can be done with it. It is very likely that you will see some kind of profound behavioral change in your child following such an event. If he was tense, for example, that might ease significantly.

Watch for humming—it's a good sign

If your child begins to hum during the massage, stay on the part where he started humming until the humming stops or you feel it is enough. This is a very good sign that means he is joining in the massage—sometimes joining in the clearing, sometimes joining in the filling.

Always be aware of your child's hands

This will help you know whether an area is blocked or empty. If his hands are pulling yours away, you are probably on a block or he may be asking you to change your touch. If his hands are coming in to touch yours, you are working on an empty area.

Chapter 5

THE 12 MOVEMENTS AND YOUR CHILD'S BODY LANGUAGE

Once you have the 12 movements of the massage under your belt, you will be able to notice more of your child's reactions to each one of the movements. You've had the basics in body language as far as knowing how to recognize when your child is joining in the massage by humming, or bringing his hands in, or pulling your hands off. In this chapter, we will take you through each of the 12 movements and describe in more detail the different reactions that we have seen over the years and what they mean in terms of energy. This information will help you know whether an area is blocked or empty and how to adjust your touch to better help your child.

Remember that your child's reactions during massage aren't *behavioral* in the ordinary sense of the word. They aren't bad behavior, or negative behavior, or even conscious choices on the part of the child. They are physical reactions to your having started the energy flowing through his body. There are basically three possible ways that energy is flowing in response to your massage:

1. A burst of energy is flowing down the energy channels you are working on.

2. You are moving energy through the channel and it is hitting a block.

3. You are moving energy into an area that is empty, and it is starting to fill up.

When energy first moves freely through the channels during a qigong massage movement, the body moves; different channels trigger different kinds of movement–anything from alternating side-to-side movements of the arms, to big, swinging up and down movements of the legs. Later on, when energy flows freely without resistance, the body becomes still and quiet. When energy pushes against a block, the child's movements can become choppy and disorganized. When energy is filling in empty areas, her body becomes quiet and receptive.

The first step is noticing these different kinds of responses and realizing they are not just random. The next step is learning what they mean in terms of energy, and adjusting your technique accordingly or just continuing the movement until the child stops reacting. Once you begin to reason according to how energy is flowing in the body (down the outside from the head to the feet), you will begin to understand what the body reactions mean, and to tune your massage to work with them as they happen. This is really what qigong massage is about—working with qi-energy to help it flow in the moment.

For example, we *do not stop the massage when the child starts reacting.* Instead, we keep going, and try to figure out what is happening energy-wise. The qigong movement we are doing is causing this body reaction, and is giving us valuable information on what your child needs help with right now. You might have uncovered a block or emptiness in his energy, or you may have succeeded in getting more energy flowing down the channels.

If you have found a block, *this is your opportunity to clear it at this very moment.* If you have found an empty area, *it is available for filling right now.* If the energy is coursing through the channels, you should keep the movement going until the child's body language quiets. Then you can go on to the next movement. We want the channels to flow properly; that will help your child grow and develop into a healthy adult.

Thinking this way will allow your massage to be much more effective and your child to progress more quickly. Before we look at the massage movements individually, let's review some more general questions that come up for parents.

What does it mean if my child starts humming while I am giving the massage?

This is very common during the patting movements on the back of the body or the chest. It means that a block is clearing out and at the same time the energy and circulation in the area is opening up. The humming signals both pleasure and relief in opening up, and is your child's way of joining in the opening up process. If he is humming while you are patting over the back of his lungs, for example, you should continue the same pace of patting, but stay on that area until the humming stops. Then you should continue down and complete the movement. Be sure to come back to the same place on the next pass to see if further opening is going to happen.

What does it mean if my child's hands come in on top of mine when I am working on an area?

It means he is filling that area, and he wants you to *slow down and stay* on that area until it has filled up.

What does it mean if my child's hands push mine away while I am working on an area?

It means that your technique on that area does not fit his problem. If you are going fast and light, try filling. If he still resists, try going even faster and lighter and making several passes.

What does it mean if my child suddenly takes my hand and places it on his forehead?

This doesn't usually happen for several months and is a very good sign that the upper energy source in the brain has begun to fill. Now the brain is open to receiving more energy and blood, and within a few days you will usually see your child demonstrate a new skill or develop a sense of humor.

What does it mean when my child suddenly becomes silly and starts making lots of little jokes?

Humor is a cognitive skill—it is seeing a situation two ways, and is a wonderful sign of brain development.

Common questions related to the specific movements
Movements 1, 2, and 3

What does it mean when my child puts his head down during the massage, or arches it backwards?

It means that you are having success in getting the energy to flow down from the head through the back to the feet. Keep doing the movement until he is relaxed or has stopped arching. See if you can guide your child down onto his belly.

What if my child won't lie down for the massage?

This means that the energy is blocked somewhere in the head, and you need to keep working at getting it down. Common places for blocks are the top of the head, the ears, and the sides and back of the neck. You may need to do the massage sitting or even standing at first until the energy flows down. When the energy is flowing freely down, the child will lie down for the massage.

What does it mean if my child is hyper after his massage?

It means that you have not yet got the energy flowing down from the head. You have moved it, but it is bouncing against a block in the head, ears, or neck, and is flaring back upwards. Find where the block is, by noticing where the child is sensitive, and do many extra quick and light passes through the area to de-block it.

What if my child starts by lying down for the massage but partway through Movement 1, 2, or 3, he gets up suddenly?

This means that, as you have started his energy moving down through the layers towards his feet, it has met a block and is bouncing upwards. Pay attention to the part of the body that triggered this reaction—that is where the block is. Common areas are the ear and neck. See page 77 for more help in de-blocking ears and necks.

What does it mean if I am massaging my child while he is lying on his belly and he bends his knees and lets his heels drift upwards?

This means that there is not enough energy and blood flowing down the back to reach the heels and hold them down. You should do some extra strokes from the knees down to help the energy reach the heels.

When I do Movements 1 and 2, he raises his eyebrows, blinks his eyes, or rubs his eyes. What does that mean?

This means that the channels are activating, and you are having success getting the energy to flow down from his forehead and head in a downward direction. This is a sign of success! Keep doing the movement until he stops these reactions.

When I do Movements 1, 2, or 3, he is ticklish and laughs and wriggles. What does that mean?

This means that the channels are empty, and you *should immediately switch* to a slow pressing hand to fill them in, until he is no longer ticklish. This usually does not take more than a few days, but can take longer.

What if he will not let me touch his ears in Movement 3?

This means that either they are blocked or they are empty. Try pressing slowly on the ears. If they are empty he will allow you to do this, and energy will start filling the ears. Then continue patting down the sides of the body. If he does not allow you to press his ears, then they are blocked and you will need to deblock them. The most direct way to deblock the ears is in the next movement, Movement 4.

When I do Movement 3, he alternates moving his right and left arm and his right and left leg. What does that mean?

That means that the channels are activating down the sides of the body, and you are having success in getting the energy to flow down. Keep doing the movement until he stops the alternating movement.

Movement 4

Movement 4 opens up the ears. Remember that the energy from the ears drains down the arm and out the back of the hand.

How do I know if her ear is blocked or empty?

Your child will avoid patting on her ear in either situation. Try slowly pressing on the ear. If she likes this, it means the ear was empty and you should continue to do the slow pressing technique all the way down the side of the neck to the back of her hand many times till the area is fully relaxed and the energy has filled in. If she does not like pressing, it means her ear is blocked.

What does it mean if she refuses both patting and pressing on one ear?

This means the energy flow in the ear is blocked, and that ear is not working properly. Most commonly the right ear is blocked; sometimes both are. Sometimes the ear will be fine one day and then *not fine* another day. If this happens (and the child is not sick with an ear infection) it means that you have cleared the surface layers of the ear, and now have reached *a deeper layer* where you have found a block that needs to be cleared.

Where do all these blocks come from?

They may be the residual effect of old ear infections, toxic exposures, or trauma to the area. Your child may have been born with a weakness in this area and be more prone to infections and problems. In this case, they will need both clearing and filling on his ears.

What is the best way to de-block an ear?

The best way to de-block her ear is for one parent to pat quickly and lightly over the ear with the fingertips pointed towards the back of the head, while the second person pats quickly and lightly on the top of her shoulder until the shoulder relaxes completely. This moves the energy through the ear down to the arm. While patting the shoulder, you can intersperse several passes down the arm. When the shoulder relaxes, it means the energy is flowing from the ear and you can now do the whole of Movement 4 down to the back of the hand.

Can my child's ear be blocked and empty on the same day?

Yes. Sometimes while you are filling the ears, the child will suddenly react with pain. This means the energy has percolated inwards and found a block. You should immediately change to a fast and light patting hand in order to clear the block. After a few passes, when the shoulders are again relaxed, you can try filling again. *Sometimes several layers of the child's energy can clear and fill in one session.* Often there is a layer of emptiness under a block where energy has not flowed for some time.

Movement 5

Opens up the child to social interaction. Remember to make eye contact, smile, and talk to the child while you do this movement. The energy flow goes into the chest and up to the face. Sometimes it also goes down the legs.

What does it mean if my child looks at me and smiles when I do Movement 5?

This means that you have had success! The movement is coordinating the basic brain reflexes needed for social interaction—the ability to turn the head and face the person, the ability to make eye contact, and the ability to tune the ear to the person's voice.

What if my child doesn't look at me when I do Movement 5?

Keep trying! It doesn't always happen in the first week. You can try making more noise when you say "up, up, up" in order to attract her attention.

What does it mean if my child's lips and tongue move while I do Movement 5?

This is an excellent sign of progress. This means that energy has flowed through the chest up to the brain and is activating the area for speech in the brain. You should continue the movement until his lips and tongue stop moving. This can continue for as long as five minutes.

What does it mean if my child starts kicking his legs while I do Movement 5?

This means that the energy is flowing from the chest down the legs, and he is integrating his arms with his legs. You should go slower and continue the movement until his legs stop kicking.

What if my child starts rubbing her eyes and yawning while I do Movement 5?

This means that you are activating the self-soothing capacity in her chest, a good sign of progress. Continue the movement gently a few more times.

What are some common mistakes in technique on Movement 5?

There are several:

- Holding the hand by the fingers instead of extending your grip to the palm leaves the child's hand feeling insecure.

- Not having enough tension in the arm to extend it out fully doesn't allow the energy wave to reach and activate the chest.

- The arm should extend out to the side of the body in order to allow the energy wave to reach the chest. If you extend the arm in front of the body, the chest will again not be activated.

- If there is not enough tension on the arm as you bring it out, the wrist will bend and close the flow of energy up to the chest. The wrist should be in alignment with the arm in this movement.

Movement 6
Stimulates the lips and tongue for speech.

What if my child's fingers are ticklish or painful?
This means that the channels to the fingers are empty, and you should immediately switch to a pressing technique. It is also very helpful to have the other parent rest a quiet hand on the center of your child's chest. This works to fill the energy to the fingers from the chest.

What if, even with pressing, my child's fingers are still uncomfortable?
You can open up the energy flow to the arm by gently kneading the front part of the armpit until it relaxes, and then pressing down the arm to the hand several times before you try pressing the fingers.

What does it mean if my child's lips and tongue move while I do this movement?
It means that you are having success stimulating the energy flow to the area of the brain responsible for speech! Keep doing the movement until the movements of the lips and tongue stop.

If your child can understand you, but isn't speaking yet, you can do lots of extra repetitions of Movement 6 throughout the day to help her start speaking.

What if my child kicks his legs wildly while I massage his fingers?
This means the long channels that run from the tips of the fingers to the tips of the toes are activating and starting to work together. Continue to massage his fingers until the leg movements stop.

What does it mean if my child starts getting sleepy while I am massaging her fingers?

This means that energy is now flowing deep into the chest around the heart, activating your child's ability to self-soothe. It is a good thing! Keep massaging the fingers for a while.

Movement 7

Activates your child's self-soothing ability.

What does it mean if my child yawns and rubs his eyes while I do this movement?

It means that you are having success in activating his ability to self-soothe. This is important both for winding down to go to sleep and for being able to tolerate transitions and changes in routine. Keep doing Movement 7 several more times.

What does it mean if my child starts burping or coughing when I do this movement?

It usually means that there is a block below the diaphragm in the belly and that Movement 5 is pushing energy against the block. You should stop Movement 7 and go on to Movement 8 in a counterclockwise direction to relieve the block. After the block in the belly has cleared, Movement 7 should not provoke coughing or burping. In the case of chronic constipation, the belly can take several weeks to clear.

What does it mean if one area of my child's ribs seems to be stiffer than another?

Usually this means that there is a block in the energy underneath. It could be the lungs—this is common in cases of asthma. If the stiffness is over the right lower ribs, there could be some congestion in the liver, and if it is stiff over the left lower ribs, there could be congestion in the stomach and spleen. You can clear the congestion in the lungs by doing Movement 2 over the back of the chest, and you can clear the congestion in the organs of the belly by doing Movement 8 on the belly counterclockwise.

Movement 8

This movement clears and strengthens the organs in the belly. Remember that the belly clears down the legs to the ground and that Movements 8 and 9 are very connected. Also remember that the clockwise movement is filling and the counterclockwise movement is clearing.

What does it mean if my child won't lie on his belly?

It usually means that there is a block in the belly that you will have to release with counterclockwise massage.

What does it mean if the child starts wriggling and reacting, and drawing up his legs when I "stir" counterclockwise on the belly?

This usually means that you have encountered a block in the belly and the blockage is having a hard time reaching his legs to release. You should stop Movement 8 on the belly, and pat quickly down Movement 9 several times until his legs relax down flat. Then go back to doing counterclockwise on the belly. If the legs draw up again, repeat Movement 9 again several times. You will know the belly is clear for the day when you can do three sets of nine circles counterclockwise without him reacting. This does not mean that it will still be clear tomorrow; there are many layers in the belly.

What does it mean if my child starts kicking his legs when I do the belly?

It means that the energy way is open from the belly to the legs and that block is clearing down from the belly to the legs. By kicking, the child is helping the block go out.

What does it mean if the child gently draws up his legs when I am going clockwise on the belly?

By gently drawing up his legs, he is creating a way for energy to pool in the belly as you are sending it inwards with your clockwise movement. This means that he is helping you with the filling part of Movement 8, and you are having success in helping energy to fill up his belly.

How can I make my Movement 8 more effective?

When you do the clockwise part of the movement, focus your intention on sending the energy inward in a spiral, and *slow down your hand*. When you do the counterclockwise part of the movement, focus your intention on drawing a spiral of energy up and out of the belly, and *move your hand faster*.

What does it mean if my child pushes my hands away when I do his belly?

This means that you have encountered a block and should switch to counterclockwise movement to clear the energy block. If you are already going counterclockwise, speed up, and take the energy down the legs using Movement 9.

What does it mean if my child puts his hands on top of mine when I do his belly?

It means that his belly is filling and he is helping you. Slow down the movements, both clockwise and counterclockwise, while he does this.

What does it mean if she makes a low-pitched noise while I am doing her belly?

It means that the lower dantien is actively filling. Keep doing the movement slowly and with a clear intention to fill until she stops making the noise. The lower belly center is very important for physical health and vitality, and this is a sign that your child will have better health and vitality in the near future.

Movement 9

Clears the energy of the belly down to the ground. It is very important that this pathway be open for the child to be able to get rid of toxins.

What do I do if my child is ticklish and wriggly when I do this movement?

This means that the channels of the front of the legs are empty, and you should immediately switch to a slow and pressing technique to help energy fill in the legs.

If they are very empty, the child can benefit by having the slow pressing massage down the legs several times a day. You can also help fill up the legs by having the other parent place a hand gently on the lower belly while you work on the legs.

Movement 10
This movement brings the energy of the front, back, and sides of the body down to the ground.

What do I do if he is ticklish or wriggly when I do this movement?
This means the channels are empty. It is often the case if there is a block in the head or neck that there is emptiness below. You should immediately switch to slow and pressing strokes.

How many times do I do this movement?
Do it until the child's legs are loose and relaxed in your hands.

Movement 11
This movement clears all the channels of the legs. Emptiness of the toes reflects emptiness of the lower belly energy source.

What do I do if the child won't take off her shoes and socks?
This means the toes are extremely empty and it may take several months for them to fill up. If your child refuses to take her shoes and socks off, you can press her toes through her shoes for the first few weeks. The toes are usually the last part of the body to fill up completely.

What do I do if her toes are ticklish?
You should immediately switch to pressing the toes to fill them. You can also have the other parent put a quiet hand on the lower belly while you do the toes to help fill them from above.

What if pressing her toes is not enough and she wriggles away from you?

Do the bicycle. Follow her leg movements and guide her into a bicycle movement. Using the big muscles of her legs in the bicycle movement will send the blood and energy to her toes. As she kicks the bicycle downward, press the energy into the toe. Move to the next toe as she draws her leg upward.

Movement 12

This movement sends nourishing energy (also known as yin energy) up inside the body to fill the three dantien of the belly, chest, and head.

What if my child's neck is cocked to one side while I am doing Movement 12?

This will prevent energy from flowing up into the head, and you should ask someone to gently hold his head in a neutral position while you do this movement.

After you have finished nine repetitions of Movement 12, don't forget to ask your child if he wants more. If he does, repeat as many sets of the nine movements as he wants.

What if my child's feet are too uncomfortable to do Movement 12?

You can try doing the movement with your palms resting against his soles, and your fingers curved over his toes. This puts less pressure on the sole of the foot.

Why should I let my child lie quietly after I finish Movement 12?

If she is lying quietly, it means that her brain is integrating the treatment you have just given her. Let her take as long as she needs to integrate it. She will get up when she is ready, or drop off to sleep.

Chapter 6

TROUBLESHOOTING

Before you look any further...

The most common mistake is to start Movement 1 too far back on the head. If you miss the right spot, there is a good chance you will have problems with the whole massage. The patting at the top of the head opens the connection between the brain and the outside world. Patting anywhere else on the head is not qigong, it is just patting. It is like trying to air out the house by blowing air on the outside of the house without ever opening the doors or windows.

If your hand position is correct in starting Movement 1, then it may be that your child's head is simply too uncomfortable to touch—he already has a feeling of pressure in the head, and touch just increases the sense of pressure. If that is the case, you can release the pressure using an extra technique to open up the energy flow down through the neck. The technique is demonstrated in the videos—just tap lightly and quickly where the skull meets the neck with all your fingers, for a minute or two, until you begin to feel the muscles soften. After that, you can do Movements 1 and 2 beginning at the neck for a few massages. After a few days, your child will usually be able to tolerate touch on the head, and you will be able to start Movements 1 and 2 in the usual place.

The ears and neck—common problem spots

The ears are almost always a problem spot for children with autism. Children who have had a lot of ear infections or who have language delays often have a great deal of difficulty around the ears during the initial massages. This is because the ears are blocked—not the ear canal itself!—in the channels that provide energy to the area. These blocks are very uncomfortable and when moving energy starts bumping up against them, pressure will build. Considering that other sensory openings in the head can also be blocked, the work around the head and neck can be challenging until the blocks begin to clear.

While our first impulse is to abbreviate the attention to this area and plunge forward into the rest of the massage, it is counterproductive to do so. Remember, a reaction means you have found a place that needs help. And, in the case of the head, if you don't get the top of the head opened and the energy flowing down in the first few movements of the massage, you won't have a lot of success with the rest of it. Will you be able to clear all of these blocks the first time? It's unlikely. You just have to do as much as feels right to you on any given day. For some, it takes several weeks even with professional help. But the key is to keep working at it. Every small bit you are able to clear will make the next amount you clear possible. So, even though you don't see the results immediately, know that you are laying the groundwork so that future work will yield results you can see.

The first step when working around the ears is to be sure that your hands are gently cupped and that your fingers are apart. A flat hand to the ear will be very uncomfortable. You also don't want to force air into the ear, so be sure that your fingers have a little space between them so air moves between them. If you are facing your child, your fingertips will naturally land on the points behind and below the ear that open up the ear.

FROM PARENT REPORTS

Month 1:

First week: This is exhausting.

Second week: I'm beginning to think I'm crazy for trying this.

Third week: Am I imagining the improvement I see?

Month 4: My stress level is down. I've had a few minutes to myself and to connect to my other children and with my husband.

Month 5: Week 1 feels like a long time ago. And I never have to go back!

Discomfort at the ears is an indication of a block or of emptiness. In the case of the ear, we don't always get a ticklish response to an emptiness, so the key is to find out where the problem lies. A quick test is to slowly press on the ear. If your child likes this, it means the ear is empty, and instead of patting the ear and then patting down the body, use the pressing motion all the way through the movement. When your child relaxes, you can move on. If she doesn't like the pressing, then the ear is blocked. Go with quick, light patting.

If the patting and the pressing are both problematic—and if your child is not ill with an ear infection—you are dealing with a block that needs to be cleared.

We often find that the right ear has more problems than the left. Whichever ear has more problems should get more of your attention. Let your child's reactions guide you to give each side what it needs. You might also find that an ear is fine one day and blocked again the next. This is actually a good sign. It means you've successfully cleared the surface channels and are now addressing the deeper layers. Use the same techniques and know that you are making progress.

Because the blocks at the ears can be stubborn, it can help in Movement 4 if one parent pats the ear while the other parent pats quickly and lightly on the top of the shoulder and makes several passes down the arm. There is a good demonstration of this in the online materials that accompanies this book. When the shoulder relaxes, it is a sign that the energy is flowing more freely from the ear. You can then try to do the entire movement. It should be much better.

Sometimes, if you are gently pressing on the ears because they are empty, your child might suddenly react in pain. This can surprise a parent who feels that the filling is going well and that the child is enjoying the feeling. You haven't done anything wrong; it just means that the energy has percolated inwards and bumped against another block. Switch to patting until the block clears and then you can switch back to filling again. You can sometimes progress down several layers in one area during a single massage. If you run into a block and clear it, you are opening up areas that might have not had a flow of energy for a very long time. Fill them up and see what happens! If your child indicates that it is time to move on by removing your filling hand, be glad for what you've accomplished. If you run into another block, however, keep going. Clear it and fill it. You should see some positive changes in your child soon.

You can sometimes clear and fill several layers in one session. If you are filling and run into a block, clear it and resume filling.

Your child's resistance to the massage

If you feel that your child's resistance is deeper or stronger than simply voicing objections and slight discomfort, i.e. the resistance is more problematic, there are several things that might be going on. You need to analyze what is behind the resistance and respond appropriately. Here are some things to consider.

Fight or flight

If you have reason to believe you've activated the child's fight or flight response—he is screaming or violently resisting—don't try to do the massage. Regularly work on starting Movement 1—at least a few times daily—but don't make a big deal of it. Start patting from the neck down when he is distracted and relaxed, and see how far you can get. Eventually, you will get farther, but take it slowly and a step at a time. It will not help, and in fact it will set you back, if you insist on doing the massage when he is adamantly refusing.

Avoidance without agitation

If your child runs away from the massage, but isn't necessarily agitated, it will help to have both parents involved. One can contain the child on his or her lap while the other does the massage. It's okay if you have to follow the child around the room while you give the massage for the first week or so.

The child refuses to lie down

When a child refuses to lie down on her belly for the massage, it can mean there is a block in the belly. You might need to start the massage with Movements 8, 9, and 10, and clear the belly before you start with Movements 1–12.

Another reason the child may refuse to lie down is that there is still a block in the head, and energy is not able to flow down. In that case, you can do the massage standing up, or sitting. Once the child starts to relax downwards, you will be able to guide her onto her belly.

Resistance in toddlers

A toddler's will is just emerging and is extremely strong. Autism puts a toddler's energy under a lot of pressure, and it isn't uncommon for him to complain loudly about your first attempts to give the massage. We have found that most toddlers will put up quite a fuss for the first week or so, but the fuss is mostly vocal, not fighting with arms and legs. As long as her body is relatively quiet—and relative is an important word when talking about toddlers being still—this is her *will* expressing itself, not her fight or flight response kicking in. In this situation, one parent holds her gently in position while the other does the massage.

Support him, encourage him, tolerate his complaints, and, most important of all, keep going! It will get easier.

Agitation and refusal

Several things can be at work here. It can be something you are doing, or it could be the state of your child. Ask yourself the questions below.

Are you doing the massage correctly?

Be sure to go through the Movement Troubleshooting Checklist in Appendix A again with somebody watching you. Ask the person you practiced with if the massage was relaxing and enjoyable. Listen carefully. Maybe you are patting too hard or with a flat hand. Try patting faster and lighter, or if that doesn't help, go with slow pressure. Watch the video again and pay close attention to the weight of hand being used in the motions.

Are you calm and relaxed when you give the massage?

Don't forget the first two steps of preparation for the massage each day: the physical and emotional self-assessment. If you are ill, exhausted, upset, tense or angry, this will communicate itself to the child, and a good massage will not be possible.

Is your child fearful?

This is a difficult situation for both the parents and the child. A fearful child needs extra support to feel safe, and it will take some extra patience to get your child to the point of relaxation and enjoyment with the massage. Hang in there. In the meantime, try these suggestions:

- Give your child more support by having one partner hold her gently while the other does the massage. This can be sitting in a lap with arms wrapped around her. Nestling against somebody's chest can be very comforting. You will know the best way to help your child feel safe enough to accept the massage.

- Ask your partner to press gently on the top of the child's head with a pulsing movement while you give the massage.

In both cases, massage over the top of the holding parent's hands, so as not to disrupt the energy flow of the movement.

Is your child particularly sensitive?

Hypersensitivity can be a sign of emptiness in a channel. It requires a different hand technique. Instead of patting, try gently pressing through all of the movements until your child begins to tolerate patting. Ultimately you want his body to be able to tolerate gentle patting, but you will have to work your way up to that.

Is your child completely unable to accept the massage?

If your child is not in the fight or flight state and you are patting as quickly and lightly as you can, but still can't tolerate the massage, her head might be extremely blocked. Until you have it more open, it will be difficult to complete all 12 massage movements.

A blocked child gets a lighter, quicker patting motion.

An empty child gets a slower, pressing hand.

Try the following approaches, one at a time:

- Start Movement 1 at the base of the head, trying to clear some of the blocks there and below before going back to the top of the head.

- Do the first part of Movement 1 in the air above the head, and continue down on the body for the first week (see video example).

- For the first week, limit the massage to the first three movements, and do them several times a day, quickly and lightly.

- Try it while he/she is watching a DVD. Break the massage up into parts.

- Try doing the massage while the child is asleep, omitting Movement 5, as it will wake her up.

Are you hesitant or fearful about the massage?

Starting any new program that impacts your child's health and well-being can be anxiety-producing, especially when the outcomes are, literally, in your hands. It is true that not all families will see significant change in their child, so you are taking a risk that it won't work, but most families will see visible improvement. Your child will react in ways that might surprise you at the time, but you needn't fear these reactions. Be gentle, don't massage through fight or flight, be in a good space to do the massage, do the massage once daily, do the movements from the top down. If you do these things, you have little to fear; you will not make the autism worse. If you don't try it, you'll never know if you could have been part of the majority of people who, after trying this program, know they have helped their child through qigong massage. For most families, even incremental improvement is well worth the effort. Imagine what significant improvement could mean.

When emotion surfaces

It is extremely hard for a parent who witnesses some kind of emotion surfacing in a child during the massage to keep going. If our child is upset, our impulse is to rush in to embrace him, to comfort him. In the case of emotions surfacing during the massage, however, it's important to continue the massage movement that triggered the response. Slow it down and stay with it until the response stops. Remain calm, and be present with your child. You can reassure him with your voice, telling him it's okay.

Think of it this way: the emotion you are witnessing is not about today, nor about the massage. It is old energy and has been blocked. To best help your child, keep doing what you are doing, without injecting your own emotion, so he can release it completely.

Once he has cleared the emotion, keep on with the rest of the massage as you would any other day. The most common emotion to be released is sorrow. For example, one of our children broke into sobs during Movement 7, and said, "I'm sorry," to his mother. They had been through a particularly long and heartbreaking journey to get the autism diagnosis. After his sorrow was released, he was much more relaxed and open. Chinese medicine says that our sorrow is stored in our lungs, and released with our tears, and so it is not unusual for an emotional release to occur during Movement 7. Another common emotion to be released is fear or shock. This often comes out when we are working on the belly. Just stay calm, and keep the circular movements going; the emotion will pass very quickly and will not return.

A reaction is your opportunity to make great strides right now!

An alphabetical list of common reactions

In some things in life, we're taught to keep going no matter what. If you studied music, dance, or acting, you are trained to pass right by the rough spot and keep going. This massage is not about that! If you get a reaction mid-movement, stop at that location and keep with it until the reaction stops. Then finish the movement.

Arms and legs alternating

During Movement 3, a child will sometimes move an opposing arm and leg together (i.e. the right arm and the left leg move, or the left arm and right leg move, at the same time). This is a good sign! The channels down the side of the body are activating and you are successfully moving energy down her body. Continue doing the movement until the response stops.

Back arches

This means that you are succeeding in moving energy from the head down toward the feet. Repeat the movement until he relaxes or stops arching. Gently guide him with your hands to lie back down.

Belly discomfort

If your child won't lie on her belly, even if you give her helping hands to get there, she probably has a block in her belly. Movement 8—and be sure to start with the counterclockwise motion—will make this more comfortable over time. In the meantime, don't force it. Just do the first three movements with your child sitting or standing.

Burping or coughing

This most commonly occurs during Movement 7. It means that energy is moving into a block in the belly. These are not blocks in the stomach or intestine per se; they are blocks to the channels that send energy to the digestive system so it can work properly. Stop the movement and progress to Movement 8, moving in a counterclockwise movement to relieve the block. After the block is clear, the coughing or burping should stop. In the case of chronic constipation, it can take several weeks for the blocks in the belly to clear.

Discomfort

Grimaces and sounds of discomfort are important indicators that you are working on an area that is blocked. It might seem hard to keep working on these areas when our instincts say to move on, but like a stubborn splinter that is not easy to remove, the block needs to clear. As a parent, you can best judge when what you are doing is too much for your child to handle; you don't want to cause actual pain or create a traumatic experience. Still, if a spot is extremely uncomfortable for a child, it is better to stay on it if you can, tapping quicker and lighter, rather than to move on without addressing the area at all. Although you might have to initially address a spot with an extremely light, rapid touch so that the discomfort for your child is minimal, know that, over time, you will be able to pat down to deeper layers as the surface layers clear.

Ears

Ears are one of the most common problem spots because there is often a lot of blockage in the head, and also emptiness. If your child won't let you tap on the ear area at all, try gently pressing on the ears. If the ears are empty, your child will allow this and your energy will start to fill the empty area. Press the ears and then pat as you go down the rest of the body. For additional detail, see the special discussion on ears on page 85–87.

Eye rubbing

If, during Movements 1 or 2, your child raises his eyebrows, blinks his eyes, or rubs them, it means you have succeeded in moving energy down from the forehead. Congratulations! Stick with whatever you are doing, with extra movements if necessary, until the reaction stops. If you are doing Movement 5 or 7 when this happens, it means you are activating the self-soothing capacity that helps with transitions and going to sleep.

Feet

It isn't uncommon for a child to refuse to take his shoes and/or socks off for the massage. This simply means that her feet are particularly sensitive and she's trying to protect them. The sensitivity comes from an extreme emptiness in the toes which can take several months to fill as the toes are usually the last area to fill up. At first, press the toes through the shoes or socks—however far you can get toward the goal of bare feet easily. Encourage the child to take off shoes and socks each time, but there is no need to fight or be forceful; if her feet are that sensitive, the skin-to-skin touch would be too much for her, anyway. Just press as well as you can, try to move toward softer shoes for the massage, and stick with it. It will change. If you can't hold the feet properly yet for Movement 12, try resting your palms on the soles of the feet and curving the fingers over the top. (See also "Ticklish" on page 97.)

Fingers ticklish or painful

As with the ears, and any other areas, the fingers can be both blocked and empty, and pain or ticklishness can be indications of either. If the fingers are ticklish, revert to the pressing technique instead of the massaging movement. Just wrap your hand around each finger, one at a time, and press it gently. Press as long as it feels good to your child. If the fingers (and it might be different for different fingers or different hands) are painful and sensitive even to the pressing, you need to clear the blocks. Try gently kneading the front of the armpit until it relaxes, press down the arm to the hand several times, and then try the fingers again. You might find that you have alternating reactions to blocks and emptiness to deal with. Just respond to your child's reactions with pressing or light massage as needed (press for ticklish, rub for blocks). Over time, the blocks and emptiness will subside and you will be able to do the massage normally.

Hands

If your child puts her hands on yours during the massage it can mean one of two things:

- If her hands are gently placed on yours, the area is filling. *Slow down* and *stay* on that area until it has filled. Your child will let you know when it's time to move on. If she puts her hands on yours during Movement 8, when you are rubbing her belly, slow down both the clockwise and the counterclockwise motions. Sometimes, several months into the program, a child will suddenly place her parent's hand on her forehead. This is a wonderful sign that means her brain has begun to fill. If this happens, stay with it and let her fill up. Watch over the next few days. She will probably demonstrate a new skill or will develop a sense of humor.

- If her hands push yours away, either your touch is wrong or you are on a block. Pat faster and lighter, but stay on the area unless you are triggering a violent fight or flight response. If you are working on the ear when you get this response, pat the ear and the top of the shoulder at the same time or try patting down the arm several times starting just below the ear. Then pat around the ear again.

- If you are rubbing on the belly in Movement 8 when your child pushes your hands away, either switch to the counterclockwise movement if you are going clockwise, or make your clockwise motion faster and then pat the energy down the legs as you would if you were doing Movement 9. You might have to rub and pat, rub and pat, several times before the block clears.

Humming

If your child begins to hum during the massage, this means that a block is clearing and, at the same time, the area is filling. This is most common when you pat the back or the chest. The humming signals both your child's pleasure and relief in opening up. The humming is his contribution to that good feeling. As long as he is humming, important things are happening. Continue patting in the same area until the humming stops and then continue the movement. Be sure to repeat the movement again, spending a little extra time at the same spot to see if there is more to be done there.

It is interesting to note the pitch of your child's voice as he hums. Don't be surprised if you hear a high pitch for a block around the head, a medium pitch at chest level, and a lower pitch if you are working on the belly.

If you are rubbing the belly and your child starts with a low-pitched hum, go nice and slow, staying with the same direction until the noise stops. The belly dantien holds an important reserve of energy for the body. When it fills, there is generally enhanced vitality or health soon to follow.

Hyper after the massage

If your child is hyper after the massage, it means that the energy is not flowing down from the head yet. You have moved it during the massage, but it is flaring back up and bouncing back against the block(s) in the head, ears or neck. Find where the block is by tapping lightly until you detect where your child is sensitive. Make several light and quick passes down through the area to de-block it.

Jumping up during the massage

If your child started the massage lying down, but then suddenly jumps up, it means that you have succeeded in getting the energy moving down through the layers, but it has encountered a block and is bouncing back. Concentrate your massage on the area that triggered the response until you can guide her back to lying down.

Kicking legs

This is different than the knees gently bending and the heels floating up; there is more energy to this response, but it is not kicking in a fight or flight way. During Movement 5, when you are working on the arms, kicking legs means your child is integrating the connections between her arms and legs. This is a good sign. The energy is flowing from the chest down. Slow down a little as you go through the movement and just keep doing it until the reaction subsides. If you are doing Movement 8, it means that the block is clearing from the belly down the legs and your child is helping to move it out.

Knees bend during movements when on her belly

There isn't enough energy flowing down from the back to reach her heels, causing them to drift up. Do some extra strokes from the knees down until her heels can stay down.

Legs draw up toward the chest

This most commonly happens as you rub the belly during Movement 8. Your response depends on which direction you are "stirring" when the legs come up.

- *Counterclockwise*: During the counterclockwise part of Movement 8, there can be some discomfort if there is a block in the area of the belly. It is common for the child to draw her legs up toward her chest if this is the case. If this happens, it means the energy needs to be moved down her legs before you continue. Stop Movement 8 and pat down her legs several times as in Movement 9 until her legs relax flat. Then go back to doing the counterclockwise motion on the belly. You might have to repeat this process several times—start the counterclockwise motion, pat down the legs, resume the counterclockwise, pat down the legs, try the counterclockwise, pat down the legs, etc. Know that this is all doing something. You know you've released the block when you can do three sets of nine circles going counterclockwise without a reaction. Unfortunately, there are many layers of the belly and you might have to do the same thing again tomorrow or another day, but look at it as a sign of progress. If the blocks are there, you want to move through them all over time.

- *Clockwise:* The legs coming up during the clockwise motion means that your child is trying to pool energy in her belly reserves as you send it inwards with your clockwise "stirring." This is a good sign that you are successfully helping that area to fill. Your child's legs coming up are a way for her to help you.

Lips and/or tongue move during a movement

Especially when you are doing Movement 6, which opens up your child's social abilities and makes the connection between the physical ability to speak and the speech centers in the brain, these movements of the tongue and mouth are reasons to celebrate. You are watching the connections happen before your eyes. Keep repeating the movement you are doing until the response stops. This can sometimes be as long as five minutes, but it is a very exciting and fruitful time.

Ribs stiff

Sometimes during Movement 7, a child will have less flexibility in the rib cage in one specific area. This can mean there is a block in the area beneath the ribs. It can be the lungs, which is common if your child has asthma. Or if the area is on the lower right rib cage, it could be the liver, or if on the lower left, the stomach and spleen. If you suspect the lungs, do more of Movement 2 over the back, concentrating at chest level, always moving the energy down the body the rest of the way. If you are concerned about a block in the liver, stomach, or spleen areas, begin in the counterclockwise direction when you get to Movement 8.

Ticklish

A ticklish spot is a sign that you've hit an empty area. Immediately switch from patting to a slow pressing hand for that area. It might take a few days before you can switch back to patting that area, but stick with the pressing motion until the ticklishness resolves. Almost all of the movements can elicit this ticklish response. If there is a lot of emptiness in the head and neck, you'll often find more ticklishness throughout the body. If it occurs during Movements 9, 10, or 11, it can help the legs and toes to fill if one parent places a hand gently on the lower belly while the other uses pressing motions to complete the movements. If you are pressing on ticklish toes, and your child still can't tolerate it, try holding her heel in one hand and moving the leg in a bicycling motion while you press with the other hand.

Yawning
Same as eye rubbing (see page 93).

Always another chance
It will take a while for all of these details to become second-nature for you. That's why, as a rule of thumb, we always say to keep with the movement you're doing and to stay calm when you get a response during the massage. Keep this book nearby so you can easily look things up. If you have another parent doing the massage with you, you can talk things over as you go and one of you can look things up while the other continues calmly working with the child. While it is important that you diligently try to learn as much as you can from this book and that you refresh your knowledge by reading it repeatedly in the first few weeks, you can't expect yourself to know everything at first. If you missed a response and you didn't get to deal with something in the optimum way on a certain day, *your child will always give you another chance!* Obviously, we want to seize opportunities to clear blocks or fill emptiness as they present themselves. This is what makes the massage effective. But, it will take time for all of this to become second nature. In the meantime, relax and enjoy the time with your child.

If you are conscientiously approaching the massage program, it will be fine, and you will get another opportunity to do the work that is needed for your child. After all, if the block is still there, it is still there. You can clear it another day.

Ask for help
If you find that you are unable to get the massage into the daily routine, and you have read the book carefully and tried the things we suggest, then it may be time to contact the QST Institute to see whether it is possible to bring a parent training to your area. Ideally, parents learn this massage program from a QST trainer and get individual help as they encounter the difficulties with their child. If you simply can't get it into the routine for the five months that it takes to bring healing, then perhaps it is time to call for help.

Chapter 7

EXTRA TECHNIQUES TO HELP YOUR CHILD GET THROUGH THE DAY

Once you have been giving the massage for a while, and your child's body and energy are accustomed to calming down with it, you will be able to use the three extra techniques described below to help your child get through the day.

A technique to help with transitions

When a child with severe autism has to leave a task behind to transfer to a different activity, he feels upset and doesn't want to do it. Unlike most children, who can move to another activity with only a little urging, there is real difficulty for the child with autism to make the dozens of changes and transitions required by daily life. To ease this, you can use your support hands in a very specific way. Before talking to your child to help him understand that there is a new activity awaiting, place one palm against his back and one over his heart. Hold him gently until you feel him notice you. Apply gentle pressure to his chest—this will calm him. Then tell him the change you want him to make. Give him a choice about whether he needs help to make the change—if he doesn't respond, use gentle pressure from your hands to physically guide your child toward the new activity. Once he sees it and engages with it, you can release him. This is a loving, effective way to reduce the struggles over day-to-day transitions.

A technique to help your child settle down when he is starting to wind up

We learned about this one from a parent who described standing at the bus station with her son, waiting for the school bus to arrive. The longer they stood there, the more he started to wind up. Suddenly, she had the idea to start tapping on his head where Movement 1 begins. After about a minute, to her surprise, he began settling down. Since then, we have seen this technique work hundreds of times. Sometimes the parent finds that the tapping should be of medium speed, and sometimes they find it works better for it to be a slow pulsing pressure. Next time your child is starting to wind up, try it, and see for yourself.

A technique to help your child focus on you when he is sitting on your lap

We found this one by accident. A father had placed his son on his lap facing him while waiting for the massage. His son was off in his own world. With a gently cupped hand, his father began patting the area at the back of the neck where the skull and the neck meet. This is the location of the point which sends circulation into the part of the brain which coordinates making eye contact and paying attention. Within moments, the son looked up into his father's eyes, smiled, and kissed him. As his father continued to softly pat the area, his son smiled and kissed him several more times.

Using qigong massage to make a hard day better

If your child is upset or is having a bad day, give her an extra massage. Just take a few deep breaths, calm yourself and start. Although it can take a few weeks to get to the stage where your child relaxes during the massage, you'll find that once you have arrived at that stage, most children will settle down by the time you've made it through the first three movements. When you are finished, it's like restarting a computer. You get to begin again with a more relaxed child.

Doing individual movements from the massage during the day is not a substitute for doing the entire massage, in order, every day. Extra movements are fine, and can be wonderful tools, but it takes the work of the whole massage daily to make your child better.

Ideas for integrating "extra" repetitions into the day

When a child is exhibiting emptiness in an area during the massage, it can be nice to take opportunities during the day to fill that area. If your child is understanding speech, but not yet talking, you've probably noticed emptiness during Movement 6 and are having to press his fingers instead of rubbing them during the massage. Or, maybe the tops of his legs are ticklish during Movement 9. You can use a calm relaxed time, such as watching "Mr. Rogers" together, to quietly sit and press his fingers and the tops of his legs. It will help to fill those areas and advance the massage process. And, as a bonus, it can be a happy, nurturing time to spend together.

Again, it is only necessary to do the massage correctly once a day in the proper order for it to work, but once parents begin to see what it is doing for their child, they are often excited and want to support that progress at other times as well.

Chapter 8

THE HEALING PROCESS

What to Expect

There is a lot of information in the preceding chapters about responses *during* the massage that indicate it is working. But what can parents expect to see in terms of behavior, health, sociability, and learning as a *result* of this work?

Humans are complex organisms with many layers. Just like an onion, you might peel off one layer, only to find another underneath. This is true whether we speak in terms of personality and emotion, or whether we are talking about the energy layers in our bodies. Your child might have dozens of layers to go through, with blocks to clear in each. Or your child might not have so many layers to address, but instead has some very stubborn blocks in a layer that might take many massages to get through. It all depends on the child and how he got to where he is. The point is, if you are correctly doing the massages every day, each massage is moving you toward real progress that will spill over into your daily life.

We hear often from parents whose children are making great strides after beginning the qigong massage treatment. Over and over, parents tell us that because their children often make sudden significant progress after they start the qigong massage, they have to keep on their toes to keep adjusting their parenting styles. Over time, the qigong will unlock many layers in addition to the surface senses and all of these improvements will eventually be reflected in growth, learning, social connections, and reduction of disruptive behavior. As you can imagine, these parents report this as "a good problem to have!"

If, however, you are going several days without seeing any aspect of the massage getting easier or noticing any improvement during the day beginning to manifest in your child, then you might want to watch the video again and find someone from your support group (recommended at the beginning of this book) to go through the Movement Troubleshooting Checklist in Appendix A as you do the massage to be sure you are on the right track with the movements.

You should also look carefully at the diet issues addressed in Chapter 10. The support group is especially important if you feel you aren't getting results. Seeing the enthusiasm of the other parents grow will help you stick with the massage and maybe even help you see that you are, indeed, getting somewhere. Also, comparing notes and learning from one another will help you make your massages more effective. Keep in mind that every child is different and will progress differently. Our goal is to help you and your own child make progress. We don't claim to solve all of the problems related to autism, nor do we claim the same level of success in all children. But, we do expect that you can make *some things better*. So, if all else fails, contact us using the information in the Additional Resources on page 137, and don't give up!

In general, once a block is cleared, you are done with it. The body is ready to heal in the area you've cleared and you will begin to see results. At first, you might have so much damage to address that you don't see significant change, but hang on to the small victories, such as the legs being more relaxed during the massage, or your child being able to lie on her belly. When you've worked through enough to do the massage without struggle or discomfort for your child, and have moved into making it a relaxed, happy time together, your child's body is already well down the road to healing and you will begin to see substantial improvement in your child's well-being if you stick with it.

Naturally, we can all form new blockages through injury, illness, or toxicity. Completion of the five months of qigong massage doesn't mean your child will never have another block, or that all of her blocks are cleared. And we don't claim a cure for autism. But unless you are one of a small number of people who say it doesn't work for them, you will get relief from some of the problem behaviors, your child will open up more socially, some of the physical problems will abate, and your child will begin to learn.

In Appendix C is My Child's Developmental Milestones. This provides a place to record some important milestones and gives you a link to important checklists you can download from the website. Together, these three short records provide a helpful before/after picture and help you to recognize the real progress that has been made. There are often dramatic improvements after a major block has been cleared or an area has filled, and the vast majority of parents in our studies are effusive in their praise of the program, rattling off many milestones without even thinking of using a checklist. Nonetheless, the checklists are powerful tools and we strongly encourage you to use them.

There are several areas in which we commonly hear reports of significant improvement. Parents of children with autism are often so exhausted that the idea of taking any one problem off the list gives them a gleam of hope. In our studies, we generally see improvement in all four areas of autism. Every child is different—some are more affected than others—and qigong isn't a magic cure-all. As the massage begins to remove some of the barriers to your child's development, however, you will see improvements in one or more of the following areas:

- sleep improves (especially falling to sleep)
- constipation or diarrhea abate
- appetite is better and range of foods increases
- tantrums are fewer and of less intensity and duration
- night terrors cease
- head-banging stops
- language processing improves and recognition and response to her name begins
- toilet training progresses
- eye contact increases
- speech develops or improves and a sense of humor evolves
- sensory ranges (over- or under-sensitivities) become more balanced
- aggressive behavior subsides
- general physical health improves, there are fewer ear infections, and asthma improves
- weak legs strengthen
- social bonds develop or improve
- the child begins to learn.

Three common and predictable reactions

There are three common and predictable reactions to the massage that are important signs of progress. They involve the following areas:

- digestion
- restored sense of pain
- onset of the "terrible twos."

Digestion

It is common for a child to pass a *strong-smelling, green-black poop* within a few days of beginning massage. If you weren't sure you were making progress before, this will definitely prove that something is happening! This is an indication that old, stagnant bile is clearing out of the liver and that the intestines are working better. It might happen only once or twice, but in cases of a heavy toxic load, it might happen many times over the first month. It is always a good thing. Thanks to your massage, your child is ridding his body of something he's been unable to release before.

Restored sense of pain

Your child might cry *for the first time* as a result of being injured. This is a wonderful sign. Although we don't like to see our child feel pain, it is normal that he feels it and cries in response. Without the ability to feel pain, a child cannot develop empathy toward others. And a child who can feel pain can also begin to feel pleasure in being gently held or touched. We often hear that the child opens up socially in significant ways soon after she begins to register pain more normally. While feeling pain for the first time is a huge milestone, be aware that your child will be flooded for a time with new sensory input. She will probably pass through a period of being hypersensitive to touch. Be patient with this; it will pass. In the meantime, continue the massage but go slower and with a pressing touch. The shell around your child is gone, but what was underneath wasn't getting nourished and now needs to be filled before she can be comfortable.

Onset of the "terrible twos"

Many children with autism are stuck at a developmental age between 18 and 24 months. Transitioning into the terrible twos, where they are strongly asserting their will and want things their own way, is a sign that they are beginning to develop socially again. Children in this phase want to do everything for themselves and practice asserting themselves by saying "no" a lot. Your child has to pass through this phase as any other child must if she is to develop appropriately. It is a real sign of progress, although it can be trying for the parents. It can also come as quite a surprise for the parents, especially if the child has always been withdrawn, to see her suddenly assertive and into everything. At this point, it is time to think about setting appropriate limits as you would with a normal two-year-old instead of being the adaptive parent of a child with autism. Give her time; she will pass through this phase as she assimilates all the new information she is getting. Just keep doing the massage.

What about regression?

As every parent of a child with regressive autism knows, regression is when a child loses skills he has previously demonstrated. All children can experience temporary regression, particularly if there is a change in their life such as a new sibling, a move, a new teacher, or a new babysitter. (Sometimes the other children in the family temporarily regress as their sibling with autism begins to improve.)

Children with autism are particularly sensitive to change in their routine and can respond by regressing. Additionally, parents report that prescription drugs, immunizations, certain foods or chemicals can also trigger a regression. Qigong neither causes regression nor prevents it. As with any child, if your child with autism regresses, you need to try to understand why it's happening and deal with the cause, if possible. The qigong can help your child cope with the stresses of the cause and help his body detoxify, but it is only a tool in this respect.

Sometimes a new behavior looks like a regression, but is really a sign of progress. There are many behaviors that the normal toddler exhibits that your child might have missed. Once she is able to learn from those experiences, you might see what seems like regressive behaviors emerge in her attempt to fill in the gaps in her development. For example, she might suddenly start lining toys up. This might look like "autistic behavior," but it might be that your child began the massage program with few, if any, fine motor skills. This is a normal way for an infant or toddler to acquire those skills. Once your child has gained the benefit from the behavior, she will stop doing it and move on to something else.

It can be hard to keep all of these developmental milestones and behaviors in mind as you observe your child, but if you can see behaviors in light of normal developmental phases that every child needs to progress through to reach the next phase, you can more easily determine if what you are seeing is regression or new learning.

The fun stuff

This chapter started with a list of areas in which you might expect improvement after a few months of doing the qigong massage. To more fully understand those changes, here is a list of more detailed indicators that show you are on the right track:

- Haircuts are no longer stressful.

- Loud noises are more easily tolerated.

- The child lets go of having to wear certain clothes every day.

- Children in diapers notice when it is wet and uncomfortable.

- More connections are made with members of the immediate family beyond the primary care-giving parent. First the other parent, then older siblings, then younger siblings. Then regularly-contacted extended family members, and, finally, teachers and the children at school.

- Those with no speech begin to indicate desires through gestures. Those who had no language at all begin to understand what you are saying and to respond to it.

- Then they begin to babble and progress to "baby talk." This is followed by single words then two- and three-word groupings.

- Bedtime is easier and sleeping through the night becomes common. Nightmares and night sweats become less frequent, then stop altogether.

- Stools that were green become brown and softer.

- Appetite for favorite foods increases and then the child progresses to being willing to try a few new things. Avoid introducing processed foods, particularly those with red dye.

- A developing sense of humor is a sign that the thinking/cognitive self is opening up. Celebrate silliness!

It's all connected

In addition to statistics and scientific confirmation that our qigong massage has had dramatic impacts, our studies have yielded some wonderful evidence that was not included in our statistical data-gathering. For example, we have found that some number of children with autism have no sense of their back. If you touch them on the back, they don't respond, and getting them to lie on their back is difficult. Over time, the qigong massage changed this.

But beyond restoring touch sensation to the back and having the child develop a conscious awareness of a part of their body they seemed to be unaware of before, an interesting thing happened. These same children—and we don't believe this is coincidental—effectively had no sense of the past. (After all, if you have nothing behind you, you have no past.) Those who were verbal couldn't tell you what they had done in school earlier that day or remember what they'd had for lunch. Obviously, discipline for somebody who can't remember what they had done or why they were being punished is difficult, not to mention the impacts of inadequate memory on learning. How incomprehensible the world must seem to a child who doesn't remember! When the channels to the back opened for these children, so did their minds. They remembered things. Imagine the ripple effect of just this one improvement. The parents would probably have been thrilled to be able to restore sensation to their child's back, but look at what they got in addition!

These connections between body, mind, and emotion are what Chinese medicine is all about. Your journey with your child will be unique to you, but don't be surprised if you, or members of your support group, report similarly exciting developments. Within two weeks of their starting the program, we have had children whose legs were weak start the massage and then learn to ride a bike; children who avoided using their hands started holding a pen and drawing; children who didn't sleep well began sleeping through the night.

The idea of taking on a five-month daily program can be daunting for the already overtaxed parents of a child with autism. And, because the changes in your child can sometimes come on rapidly, the parent also has to be aware and ready to respond to this "new child" they are parenting. It sounds hard, and the first few weeks definitely can be, but hope is invigorating, and undeniable progress is even more so. It is five months that can literally change your, and your child's, world.

Chapter 9

UNDERSTANDING TOXICITY IN CHILDREN WITH AUTISM

Prevention

To fully understand how the qigong massage will help restore more normal function to your child, it is worthwhile to know how the damage first occurred. The image of the river can help visualize how this happens.

In the case of toxicity, we know that a river can absorb some amount of toxins before it becomes severely polluted. Each river has a "carrying capacity," an ability to carry away waste and remain healthy. But if the carrying capacity is exceeded, the river becomes ill, the fish that live in it become ill, and the land around the river suffers. The river slows down and trash collects in the bends and twists, plugging the entry and exit points. The same goes for the channels in our body that carry qi-energy. These channels help our blood to bring life-giving nourishment to our cells and cleanse our bodies, carrying illness away. If they are blocked, these critical functions can't happen.

This is an important concept in understanding the toxicity that can be behind autism. A young child's "carrying capacity" for toxicity is much lower than that of an adult, and an inability to process the toxins that come into the body can have a profound effect. Fortunately, qigong massage can help clear the blocks so that, in many cases, the body can repair damage caused by toxicity.

Emptiness in the channels, or deficiency, is a second cause of autism recognized by Chinese medicine. Remember that everything in the body affects everything else. Deficiency can make the channels more susceptible to toxicity. If a river is very small, has a low flow, or has very little water in it, it will be much more susceptible to toxicity than a more robust river with a lot of flow. A child who starts life smaller and weaker than his peers due to premature birth, maternal drug addiction, or genetic disorders will have more deficiency and thus be more vulnerable to damage by toxicity.

The third contributing cause of autism is trauma or compression to the head and neck. This is less common than the other two causes, but can happen during a difficult delivery or subsequent head injury.

More than half the children we have seen who have autism came from healthy parents, were the product of a normal pregnancy and birth, and never had head trauma. The majority of these children sustained injury to their nervous system from toxicity. We cannot avoid toxins completely—they are everywhere. Fortunately we can get rid of them if we are not overloaded at any one time. That so many otherwise healthy children are getting ill with autism raises some difficult questions about how we are dealing with the toxicity in our modern world.

Toxicity is also an issue for the remainder of children with autism who were born with risk factors for autism such as large birth size, forceps or vacuum suction delivery, older parents on medications for chronic conditions, exposure to drugs or alcohol during pregnancy, etc. It takes less toxicity to exceed the carrying capacity for these children and cause blocks to their energy channels. The medical and health policy communities have much work ahead to look at how to better protect our children from the toxic loads that are making them sick.

When we consider that, according to the Eastern philosophy of disease, autism is caused by trauma, toxicity, deficiency, or a combination of the three, it is logical that we try to minimize the occurrence of these factors in our childrens' lives. Parents already work very hard to minimize injury and trauma, and so it isn't necessary to comment on those.

Don't be surprised if during the massage you notice a metallic taste or smell. These are the toxins being released from your child's body.

Toxicity, however, is a different matter. All children have less ability to deal with chemicals than adults, but one of the hallmarks of autism is a more deeply compromised ability to break down and clear toxins. And so, the child's body with autism holds onto, and reacts to, toxins in the environment that most of us, and even most children, might not even notice. The sticky, green, smelly poops that happen soon after beginning the massage program are indicators of the toxic load the child is carrying. These toxins suppress health and put a tremendous burden on his system.

And so, at the same time your child is trying to live in a world that is not being accurately represented to him by his senses, his body is trying to function while being chronically chemically impaired. It can't feel good.

By helping to keep these toxins out of your child's environment, you can not only help him to heal in the long term, but you can also avoid the immediate behavioral reactions some of these chemicals cause. Take, for example, markers. Scented markers, washable markers, dry erase markers; they fill our world. To make them dry quickly, there is a solvent added that can make a child, even those not on the autism spectrum, become temporarily hyperactive. One of the parents in our study reported that her son got into markers one day and drew all over himself. He was soon distressed and lay on the couch rocking and moaning for what turned out to be days. When he returned to school, he couldn't remember his teachers' names. The parent reports that it was a month before he returned to his normal behavior. While hyperactivity is the most common reaction we hear about markers, some children become drowsy or "out of it" for a while after using them. It's a simple thing to switch to crayons, and it's one of the first things you should do.

It is important as you read through the following that you understand that this discussion is not intended to condemn the makers of the chemicals we've come to rely on in our lives. After all, they didn't make these products with intent to harm children. It is simply that children with autism typically have such a low tolerance to chemicals that parents need to be on the lookout.

The three ways toxins enter the body

There are three main ways toxins can enter a child's body. They can be:

- ingested
- breathed in
- absorbed through the skin.

Ingesting chemicals: Foods

It is very difficult to avoid chemicals in food. Even breast milk has toxins in it, albeit at very low levels. Fruits and vegetables are sprayed with them, and processed foods are full of preservatives and dyes. Because there are many studies that point to red dyes as particularly troublesome, it is wise to get them completely out of your child's diet. One challenge that has evolved in recent years is the advent of laws that require that foods served as snacks in schools and preschools be store bought. Unfortunately, most of the foods that end up being served to our children in these circumstances are highly processed and often dye-laden. For a child with autism, especially, the chemical burden is very high.

Here are some recommendations for how to help your child reduce the toxic load through ingestion:

- Buy organic fruits and vegetables when you can.

- Become an avid label reader. Watch out for dyes and a long list of other chemicals. If there is any red dye in a food, do not buy it. The range of foods that contain red dye is surprising, but pay special attention to gelatin snacks, candy, beverages, ice creams, cheese, and cookies. Don't be discouraged; there are plenty of popular brands that do not contain dyes. Be aware, too, that some medicines (and even toothpastes!) contain dyes; ask your doctor or pharmacist for alternatives.

- Cook from scratch as much as possible to avoid the chemicals that enhance and preserve processed food.

- Take homemade snacks to preschool for your child so he can snack at the same time as other children are having store-bought snacks.

Breathing chemicals

Wouldn't it be nice if we could all spend our days near a high mountain lake, surrounded by air-purifying evergreens, or at the beach breathing in clean air from the ocean? Of course, we all know that even these environments can be highly polluted these days, but you get the idea. We live in a world where harmful chemicals and other substances are unavoidably present in the air we breathe. Mercury is emitted from the garbage burner down the road, electric power plants that burn fossil fuels emit sulfur dioxide, carbon monoxide, and a host of other unhealthy substances. The black, smoke-belching diesel truck in front of us at the stoplight signals to us that we are about to inhale something we'd prefer not to have in our lungs. We can't protect our children from all of this, nor are we suggesting that there is a specific, direct correlation between autism and the presence of these substances in our world. There are some inhaled chemicals, however, that you can remove from your child's environment.

The best tool a parent has for helping her child in this regard is her nose. If you can smell it, you might want to think about whether your child should be inhaling it. Do you, for example, really need air fresheners? Does your child react negatively on the days you clean your bathroom with various cleansers? If your child pulls away if you are close, could it be your cologne or hair spray? Is there something in the air at a relative's house that seems to set your child off? And don't forget to eliminate markers. Period.

This is not to suggest that you eliminate all the chemicals in your life that make things easier for you. Also, you can't realistically go around policing every environment before you take your child there, but do become sensitive to your child's reaction in the presence of such chemicals. If you aren't certain, remove the chemical for a while and then reintroduce it and watch for a reaction. Know that new carpet, paint, paint thinner, and construction adhesives can create major reactions, too. Additionally—and this is a hard one—analyze what is happening at your child's day care, preschool, or school. The industrial commercial cleaners and waxes used in some facilities leave long-lasting residue in the air. Ask questions, use your nose, and look for patterns.

This is clearly not going to be easy, because looking for reactions to one particular thing with a child who is reacting to things all over the place—unless she has become totally overwhelmed and shut down—takes a lot of energy. But remember, if you can eliminate an environmental cause of a troublesome behavior, you will save yourself a tremendous amount of energy down the road. And, more importantly, of course, you will have enhanced your child's well-being and comfort.

Chemicals absorbed through the skin

The parent's story about her son who drew on himself with markers is an excellent example of a toxin being absorbed through the skin. We have no evidence to point at other specific substances, but as a parent, be on the lookout for possible triggers when there is sudden, otherwise unexplainable discomfort in your child. Maybe the new clothes she is wearing have been treated somehow. Did you switch fabric softeners? (Do you need fabric softeners?) Is there scent in your detergent? Is there a behavioral reaction after you've used a lotion on your child? Certainly, don't let your child's skin come into contact with cleaning products, even the mildest of them, except for mild soap and shampoo. But even look closely at those; you might want to switch from deodorant soap to something milder.

Other ways that toxins can enter the body

Food allergies

It's odd to lump food into a discussion of toxicity, but if your child is unable to properly process certain kinds of food, the load on her body from a food she can't properly digest is similar to that of a man-made toxin.

We've already discussed the need to eliminate red dye and to avoid the other dyes and preservatives in processed foods. A food allergy goes beyond avoiding additives; it goes to a problem with a food that is otherwise considered wholesome and nourishing.

While we have not done a specific study about this in terms of autism compared to the general population, we have found a large number of the children in our studies to be allergic to wheat and milk products. There are controlled studies that verify that such allergies are fairly common in children, so we weren't surprised to see a large intolerance for these foods in the autistic children we looked at, especially considering their diminished capacity to deal with toxins in general.

The substance in milk that we find troublesome is not lactose, as you might expect. It is casein. If your child is lactose intolerant, she will have the same kind of cramping and diarrhea after eating dairy products that so many in the general population experience. In the case of casein intolerance, it's a little harder to spot.

There are five things that can indicate a gluten/casein food allergy.

- The child has a voracious appetite in the presence of foods high in wheat or dairy, such as pizza. A child might eat a huge amount of these foods and then exhibit anger when they are denied more. This is a sign that instead of creating a sense of fullness, the foods are triggering an unwanted chemical reaction in the body.

- The child wants to drink milk all day and the few foods she eats all contain milk or wheat. It is common for us to crave the very foods to which there is an allergy.

- The child easily becomes aggressive. In cases of a child who was not aggressive before his regression into autism, aggression or hyperactivity is often a side-effect of a drug, chemical, or food that he cannot eliminate from his system.

- The belly is bloated or tender to the touch. If your child won't lie on her belly, keep an eye out for other symptoms. A distended belly can be a response to a food allergy.

- The child has no language—neither speaking, nor understanding. Parents report that their child is "spaced out." Unprocessed chemicals from food allergies can knock us out just as other chemicals such as those found in medicines can.

This is not to say that all children with autism should be on a gluten-free, casein-free diet, because not all children have this intolerance. We have found that, if the intolerance is mild or moderate, an awareness of potential problems on the part of the parents results in a fairly natural reduction in troublesome foods. That often seems to be enough. This is because after a few months of the qigong massage, the child's appetite tends to open up, her digestive system works better, and she begins to enjoy eating more. As she begins to try new foods, her diet comes into better balance and her food intolerances disappear.

In the case of a severe intolerance, however, we have had significant improvements after the child begins a gluten-free, casein-free (GFCF) diet. We have had children in the study who made great strides during the first two months or so of qigong, but then hit a plateau. The tactile sensory problems and constipation might have gone and they might have begun sleeping well at night, but there still didn't seem to be any language recognition nor speech development, and the problems with aggression had not subsided. In these cases, the parents who started a GFCF diet had positive progress soon thereafter, and the positive signs during the massage and related development resumed.

There are several websites and books written about the gluten-free, casein-free (GFCF) diet if you are interested in giving it a try. It sounds daunting. After all, the typical American meal is filled with wheat and dairy: cheese, yogurt, ice cream, bread, pasta, and most snacks. It's a little easier if you think in terms of what you *can* have: rice, potatoes, beans, rice milk, meat, fruit, and vegetables. There is a lot of help available for ideas on how to make the transition. If you feel you should give it try, start with GFCF.com and branch out from there.

Vaccines

While the debate rages on in the courts and media as to whether vaccines cause autism, a growing number of physicians and parents have expressed concern that vaccines may pose a risk for autism. Many parents are choosing not to vaccinate their children, or to vaccinate them less than the recommended amount, and a number of physicians are willing to administer "lighter vaccine schedules."

The research studies are conflicted about whether there is a connection between vaccines and autism. When it comes to single vaccines, some studies say that a particular vaccine increases the risk of autism; other studies say that it does not. We are only aware of one U.S. study that has considered the impact of the whole vaccine schedule on the incidence of autism. In this study of 20,000 children, vaccinated children were found to be two to four times more likely to have autism than unvaccinated children.[1]

There is controversy on almost every aspect of this topic, but logic dictates that until scientists can agree on the causes of autism, the possibility that vaccines contribute to it must remain under consideration.

When you consider that immunizations are, for the most part, potent drugs, and that we are injecting active ingredients and preservatives into our children, the question of toxic load must be raised. Too much of any drug or preservative has toxic side-effects, regardless of age, as does taking too many different drugs at once. We know that the nervous system in an infant or small child is developing very rapidly and that children are more vulnerable to damage from chemicals than adults are, so it's no wonder that parents have questioned whether vaccines put their child at risk for autism. The people who make policy about vaccinations, makers of the vaccines, and many other health professionals deny a correlation. A little history can help illuminate why there is such a debate.

The first case of autism appeared in the U.S. in 1943. Before then, it was completely unknown. Somehow, by 2009, it was a worldwide problem with a one and a half million recognized cases in the United States alone. Something has to be causing this!

Vaccines came under suspicion because at the same time as there was an increase in use, frequency, and number of vaccinations, so too was there a striking jump in reported cases of autism.

Before 1981, the vaccine policy in the United States differentiated between "low-risk" groups who had a healthy immune system, and "high-risk" groups such as the elderly or chronically ill, who were at risk for serious complications from ordinary illnesses. The high-risk people were given extra vaccines to protect them from conditions from which people with normal immune systems could easily recover. The inconvenience of feeling miserable and missing a few days of work was not considered a reason to recommend a vaccine for everyone, and so things such as the flu vaccine were on an "optional" list. Newborns were not typically vaccinated because it was considered ill-advised given the delicate nature of the newborn's nervous system and the immaturity of their immune system.

In the 1980s, however, the policy changed. We started to vaccinate infants at birth instead of waiting until they were at least two months old, and the high-risk, low-risk, and optional lists were merged. That meant that healthy people

1 www.generationrescue.org.

began to be vaccinated as if they were immune-compromised. Flu shots were recommended for everyone, even pregnant women—a first! Newborns were given vaccines for Hepatitis B, even though it is not typically an issue until adolescence and the possible onset of sexual activity. Additional vaccines, such as the one for chickenpox, were added for the convenience of not missing work.

Once the policy changed, there was no looking back. The former "optional" list was forgotten, and everyone started getting a lot more immunizations, most of them for illnesses that are not typically life-threatening. It was then that the occurrence of autism began to move from the rate of 1 in 10,000 to the current rate of 1 in 100. As the U.S. vaccine schedule changed, the rest of the world tended to follow.

In the early 1990s there were so many cases of regressive autism, and so much concern about the cumulative effect of the mercury that was being used in the vaccines as a preservative, that the U.S. government recommended that vaccine makers remove the mercury from children's vaccines. In the U.S. and Europe, but not yet in other parts of the world, mercury was phased out and replaced with aluminum.

Here are some of the changes in our vaccine schedule over the past 30 years. Because there are so many changes, it will be a lengthy and difficult process for scientific research to pinpoint whether individual changes resulted in a risk for autism:

- In the last 30 years, the number of vaccines administered to a child before the age of three has risen from 18 to 42.

- Vaccines are more typically bundled together, meaning more potential load per injection.

- Infants are vaccinated at birth instead of beginning the schedule at two or three months.

- The preservatives are changing from mercury to aluminum.

- The formulations of live viruses and genetically modified ingredients are changing.

There is a lot of room for questions here, and until the causes of autism are clearly identified, we will not know how to prevent it, or whether vaccinations are increasing the risk of our children getting it. Given this information, what should a parent do?

The options

Parents have the right to know the facts about their children's illnesses and their treatments. They also have a right to know when there is dispute about treatments their doctors recommend. Vaccine policy in the United States, however, is fairly structured. Because there often is not a lot of flexibility built into the system, parents and others have launched websites to keep consumers abreast of recent developments in both research and law. There are doctors who are open to giving fewer vaccines in the first three years of life—parents have a right to find such doctors if they choose.

No parent wants their child to contract a preventable disease, and certainly there is a public safety benefit to vaccination in general. The hard question for parents, then, is how to weigh the risk of developing autism against the risk of contracting a serious disease?

There are also legal aspects to consider. In general, vaccinations are not required by law until your child enters preschool, or possibly even public school. Most states allow families to refuse vaccinations on the basis of religious belief or medical contraindications. Are there situations where a parent can be forced to permit full immunization of their child? In the coming years, the issue will come up in court until it is decided one way or the other.

Until then, parents are considering different options for vaccinating their children. Some parents are choosing to avoid vaccinations altogether. Others are more cautious before the age of three, asking to wait on those vaccines that aren't really necessary and opting in to only those for which the risk of infection is higher and the consequences more dangerous. Still others are going with the full vaccination schedule as recommended by the U.S. government and their doctors.

Ultimately, the permission to vaccinate a child can only be given by the parents or guardians. The best thing to do if you have concerns is to become better informed and to find a doctor who is open to discussing the options. There are a number of books on the subject and, increasingly, there are more such doctors.

Awareness not obsession

For the already stressed parent of a child with autism, the preceding information can be overwhelming. On top of everything else, where does one find the energy to reduce all of the toxins in her child's environment? The answer is: you do what you can. Remember, each child is unique and may or may not respond adversely to some of the things we listed. Also, many of the examples we used above—with the exception of red dye—are not necessarily proven to cause problems, nor do we specifically suggest that they do. We mention them only as examples to help you become aware of the number of times your child encounters chemicals in a typical day. For a child who is unable to process toxins well, as in the case of autism, this simple awareness might result in a few changes in the household that can reap huge benefits. It might not be a sensitivity to a specific substance that causes problems, but the accumulated *load* of toxins.

Also, remember that the massage is going to help your child process and clear toxins. Every parent will want to do everything they possibly can to help their child get better. At this point, be aware of the things discussed in this chapter, make the changes that work for you, but make the number one priority the massage. It must become a part of the daily routine. For most exhausted parents of children with autism, this will initially be daunting enough.

The good news is, that if you stick with the daily program, and if you are like the vast majority of families who do the program, things will get significantly easier for you. As they do, you will be better able to pay attention to these other potentially important factors. Even though the qigong massage will result in a healthier, stronger child, your child still had an overload of toxicity at some point and will remain sensitive to toxins, and subject to setbacks as a result, for many years. Eventually, his body will mature and he should be able to better handle them.

Chapter 10

A Diet for Children with Autism

When you think about the best diet for your child, there are two aspects to consider. First: What are the foods to avoid? And second: What are the foods to offer? In the previous chapter on toxicity, we have shared the information that many processed foods contain dyes and chemicals that often trigger behavioral problems in children with autism. Now we will share the How and the Why of what Chinese medicine recommends we feed our young children with autism to optimize their growth and development.

The Chinese medicine view of our digestive system is that it is like a slow cooker that cooks our food, and then extracts the nutrition from it. If we have a strong digestive system, we will have a good appetite, and normal bowels. If, on the other hand, our digestive system is weak, then we have a poor appetite, and problems with our bowels. Many children with autism have a poor appetite and eat a very narrow range of foods. Needless to say, home cooking with fresh ingredients will always provide the most nutritious food, but what more can Chinese medicine teach us about improving their appetites?

Food should be warm and cooked

If a child isn't digesting well, it will only make things worse if we give him cold and raw food. He will have to use what little digestive energy he has to warm up the food, and then to cook it. The digestive enzymes don't work at a cold temperature; they only work at body temperature. Also, just think of how long it takes to cook green beans on the stove until they are soft. Raw vegetables are hard to digest if the system is weak, which is why they often cause diarrhea or show up undigested in the stool.

Breakfast should be warm cereal. For lunch and dinner, noodles, rice, and cooked vegetables are easy to digest and nourishing. Small amounts of cooked meat provide a ready source of protein. Ripe, soft fruits or pureed fruits such as applesauce make good snacks.

If we feed our children a diet that is easy to digest, their digestive system will grow stronger, and their appetite will increase accordingly. Within a few months, parents are pleased to find that their children are eating more, and beginning to sample foods that they have never eaten before.

We have found that this advice is just as good for adults, too. If you want to slow down your metabolism and gain weight, just ice your core (your stomach) down several times a day with cold drinks and smoothies. And then ask it to digest a meal of raw salads and vegetables. This is an effective way to slow down your metabolism. If we want our metabolism to function optimally, it is best for us to take the majority of our food warmed and cooked. We can have a salad or fruits on the side, but not as a regular main course. And we can take the majority of our liquids at room temperature, or warm.

There should be a balance in the flavors of the food that is offered

The easiest foods to digest are the ones that are neutral or slightly sweet in flavor—sweet potatoes, French fries, pasta. But children need and enjoy the salty flavor as well, and will enjoy it when you use salt in your cooking. It is best to avoid the very sour and very sweet flavors that are in candies and desserts, as they tend to overpower a child's appetite and confuse his ability to choose what his body needs.

If your child has a tendency to phlegm in the chest or nose, or recurrent upper respiratory infections, dairy should be avoided

We have had many children who started our program with a continual runny nose and the tendency to a wet cough. Some of them had experienced dozens of ear infections and repeated courses of antibiotics. The vast majority of these children ended up with dry noses and a much better immune system, and a big part of their parents' success in achieving this was taking their child off milk, cheese, yoghurt, and ice cream. Parents did not find it hard to substitute the milk with rice milk, and find other sources of protein. Once the phlegm cleared up, the children's appetites improved and they ate more of what they were offered. Without the frequent antibiotics, their diarrhea resolved and their digestive and immune systems regained their health.

Chapter 11

Your Child's Program After the First Five Months

Just as each child follows a unique healing path, each child requires a different follow-up program when the first five months of qigong comes to an end. The follow-up program sets in place a safety net that aims to protect the child's gains and keep the child on a good developmental path for the years to come. Since there are no controlled studies predicting how your child will progress over the coming years, parents have to use common-sense principles, based on what they know about autism now, and then adjust the program to fit their child's changing needs as they learn more.

That said, we recommend a five-part follow-up program.

Diet

Food and drink are the physical building blocks for growth and development. As much as possible, food needs to be fresh and homemade along the lines discussed in the previous chapter. Processed foods, including red-dye containing foods, are not good for your health or that of your child and should be avoided as much as possible. By now, you might well have already tried the GFCF diet, and have seen for yourself whether your child needs this diet to function well. When special diets are working well for children with autism, parents tend to stick with them for several years after the child has stabilized—why mess with a winning combination? We agree.

Protection from toxins

Continue to be vigilant to limit your child's exposure to fumes, solvents, pesticides, and household chemicals. It may take her system years longer than other children to grow to its full strength. Until it has done so, you will need to provide extra protection.

Decide about your child's vaccination schedule

When science admits freely that it doesn't know what is causing autism, and there is serious disagreement between scientists about whether the vaccines increase the risk of autism, parents are left to come up with their own decision about vaccinating their child. Become informed. Find a doctor who will discuss the options with you. It is not all or nothing. You don't have to give all the shots right away. You can space out the shots; you can ask for fewer shots. If it is a choice between a risk of autism and a risk of missing work while your child gets over the chickenpox, consider the stakes. Parents are willing to miss a lot of work if it means their child won't get autism.

The incidence of autism is still growing. As of 2009, it occurred in one in a hundred children. Never in human history have so many children been struck with disability so young. You can't count on the experts to agree on what you should do to prevent autism. Sometimes you just have to use common sense and evaluate the risks for yourself.

Avoid unproven treatments

There are hundreds of treatments for autism advertised on the internet. Be very careful not to waste your money and risk exposing your child to drugs, supplements, and programs that might set her back. Most of the things advertised do not have a controlled study backing them. Stay away from these things. As a parent you are very vulnerable to wanting to do everything that anyone recommends and says will help, but when it comes to autism, there is so much sales hype, and so many things that carry a risk of harm, that it is better for you not to try things that have no research behind them.

Qigong massage

Qigong massage brings your child to balance every day, and puts something in his pocket to cover tomorrow's challenges and stresses. When it is done every day, it has a cumulative effect on the child and his reserves start to grow. After the first five months, we encourage parents to continue the massage and find their own pace according to how far behind their child is on the developmental checklist. Generally, we recommend keeping the massage going on a daily basis for at least a year or two or until the child reaches her developmental age.

Discontinuing the massage

Once your child is stable, there is no formal weaning process. The principle you follow is to give the massage as often as you think your child needs it, as often as she asks for it, and definitely whenever you notice her sensory reactions are out of balance. This might be once or twice a week or once or twice a month, depending on your child. One thing we have heard from parents after they stop massage is that development can slow down a tad. Be sensitive to this, and, if you notice your child is not doing as well in school, start the massage up again regularly; at least three days a week. It helps your child to function optimally.

Teachers and others

Please be very careful about who you allow to give your child qigong massage. If someone who is not connected to your child forces it on him, it can do harm. We recommend that teachers and aides who want to understand qigong better, and want to use it in the classroom with parent permission, take a course through the Qigong Sensory Training Institute (www.qsti.org) to prepare themselves.

Our final words to you

We hope that this book is helpful. We hope that it gives you what you need to learn qigong massage, and that you are able to get it into your child's routine. We hope that the massage brings more peace, love, and relaxation into your home and into your child's life. We hope that it lightens your load. Please contact us via our website www.qsti.org and give us your feedback on what worked and what didn't work for you. As much as we love the children, we did this for the parents.

Appendix A

MOVEMENT TROUBLESHOOTING CHECKLIST

The following allows you to have a partner check that you are doing the movements optimally. This is a valuable tool for a support group activity. You can use it while you practice with a partner, as you begin with your child, again after a week, and again a couple of weeks later. If you feel you aren't getting results, it could be that you are missing an important concept, such as not opening the head properly, or are tapping around the ears incorrectly, or are not appropriately adjusting the speed and weight of your hand. An observer who has read the rest of this book and is using the checklist should be able to catch those problems for you.

In addition to checking that the techniques are correct, parent support group partners can help one another maintain a cheerful, positive attitude for the massage, during the first week or so when it is roughest, and can help each other recognize and adapt to developmental strides.

The parent must ensure all of the following when doing the movements.

Movement 1

- Check that there are no hair clasps, ties or such on the head.

- Pat at the soft spot, not just patting the head.

- Do adequate pats before moving on.

- Follow the correct line down the center of the head and spine, down the middle of the back and legs to the outside of the ankles.

- Go all the way to the heels.

- Give extra pats in areas where the child's responses indicate the need (e.g. humming or discomfort).

- Adjust the weight of the hand appropriately.

Movement 2

- Begin with both hands tapping next to the soft spot on the top of the head.

- Follow the correct line on either side of the spine.

- Give extra pats in areas where the child's responses indicate the need (e.g. humming or discomfort).

Movement 3

- Begin with tapping at the soft spot on the top of the head.

- Tap several times, fingers to the back of the ears.

- Keep the fingers slightly spread and adjust the weight of tapping as appropriate.

- Tap well into the sides of the neck.

- Follow the correct path down the sides of the body to the outside of the ankle.

Movement 4

- Use the proper hand (open fingers, finger tips at the back of the ear) and adjust the weight of tapping as appropriate.

- Give the ear ample pats before moving on.

- Accommodate particular discomfort at the ear by having a partner tap on the top of the shoulder at the same time, if possible.

- Follow the correct line from ear to side of the neck, across the top of the shoulder, down the upper arm to the elbow, across the top of the forearm and to the top of the hand.

- Do extra repetitions, if possible, if the ear is blocked.

- Know when to switch to pressing.

Movement 5

- Hand position (grip) is correct.

- The child's arm is fully extended (no bend at the elbow).

- The gentle shaking creates a wave you can see clear to the shoulder.

- Makes eye contact and cheerfully speak to the child to accompany the movement (e.g. "up, up, up...down, down, down").

Movement 6

- Use the appropriate technique—rubbing or pressing—in response to the child's responses.

- Watch for responses and spend extra time on certain fingers if needed.

Movement 7

- The movement is slow and rhythmic, not rushed.

- Press gently, but firmly, moving the ribs slightly, as would happen with a breath.

- Start at the collarbone and follow to the end of the ribs.

- Watch for sleepiness or other responses, such as humming or the child's hands moving to rest on top of hers, and adjust accordingly.

Movement 8

- Consider in advance whether the child has constipation, diarrhea, or normal stools and "stir" in the correct directions.

- Make the circles around the belly button.

- Adjust speed and pressure according to the situation and direction.

- Watch for responses, such as humming or the legs drawing up, and adjust appropriately.

Movement 9

- Follow the correct line down the top of the thigh, shin, and top of the foot.

- Adjust the weight of the hand for ticklishness or other responses.

- "Pat down" the legs if they draw up and then resume the movement.

Movement 10

- Support the heel with one hand as the other starts behind the knee.

- The movements are smooth and continuous.

- The movement is continued until the leg is relaxed and the calf muscle loose.

- Know what to do if the calf is ticklish (gently squeeze down the calf).

Movement 11

- Use rubbing or pressing as appropriate.

- Adjust to a bicycling motion if necessary.

- Spend extra time if needed on individual toes.

Movement 12

- Check that the body is aligned and the neck is neutral (straight).

- Position the fingers correctly on the foot, using the alternate hold only if necessary.

- Assume a healthy back and leg posture for himself.

- Watch for a slight chin movement during the movement.

- Count slowly aloud to track the movements.

- Ask the child if she wants another set when done.

After finishing the massage

Let the child rest and integrate the effects of the massage until she chooses to get up. Once she gets up, the parent should offer encouragement and affection—the child might enjoy a quiet hug.

Appendix B

SENSORY AND SELF-REGULATION CHECKLIST

Date: _____ Name of child: _____

Name of person completing checklist: _____

Please circle the response for each item that most accurately describes your child.

1. TOUCH/PAIN

	Often	Sometimes	Rarely	Never
• Doesn't notice if the diaper is wet or dirty	3	2	1	0
• Face washing is difficult	3	2	1	0
• Haircuts are difficult	3	2	1	0
• Refuses to wear a hat	3	2	1	0
• Prefers to wear a hat	3	2	1	0
• Cutting fingernails is difficult	3	2	1	0
• Prefers to wear one or two gloves	3	2	1	0
• Avoids wearing gloves	3	2	1	0
• Cutting toenails is difficult	3	2	1	0
• Will only wear certain footwear (e.g. loose shoes, no socks)	3	2	1	0
• Prefers to wear the same clothes day after day	3	2	1	0
• Will only wear certain clothes (e.g. no elastic, not tight, no tags, long or short sleeves)	3	2	1	0
• Cries tears when falls, scrapes skin, or gets hurt (scale is reversed on purpose)	0	1	2	3

Self-regulation—attention/self-soothing/sleep	Often	Sometimes	Rarely	Never
• Has to be prompted to make eye contact when spoken to	3	2	1	0
• Stares off into space	3	2	1	0
• Does not cry tears when hurt or upset	3	2	1	0
• Seems unaware when others are hurt	3	2	1	0
• Has difficulty calming him/herself when upset	3	2	1	0
• Gets upset or tantrums when asked to make a transition	3	2	1	0
• Has difficulty falling asleep at bedtime	3	2	1	0
• Has difficulty falling back asleep when awakens during the night	3	2	1	0
• Awakens very early and stays awake	3	2	1	0
• Has difficulty awakening in morning	3	2	1	0
• Makes little jokes (*answer only if your child has language*) (scale is reversed on purpose)	0	1	2	3

2. VISION	Often	Sometimes	Rarely	Never
• Looks at objects out of sides of eyes	3	2	1	0
• Is bothered by certain lights	3	2	1	0

Self-regulation—irritability/aggression	Often	Sometimes	Rarely	Never
• Tantrums or meltdowns (tantrums last _____ minutes, and occur _____ times/day)	3	2	1	0
• Cries easily when frustrated	3	2	1	0
• Hits or kicks others	3	2	1	0
• Scratches or pulls other's hair	3	2	1	0
• Bites others	3	2	1	0
• Throws things at others	3	2	1	0
• Bowel movements are often green	3	2	1	0
• Gets aggressive or "hyper" with exposure to certain smells	3	2	1	0

3. HEARING

	Often	Sometimes	Rarely	Never
• Seems not to notice when spoken to in a normal voice	3	2	1	0
• Does not respond to his/her name	3	2	1	0
• Reacts poorly to certain everyday noises	3	2	1	0
• Covers ears with certain sounds	3	2	1	0
• Reacts strongly when others cry loudly or scream	3	2	1	0
• Is startled by sudden noises	3	2	1	0

Self-regulation—toilet training

	Often	Sometimes	Rarely	Never
• Is dry at night (scale is reversed on purpose)	0	1	2	3
• Diaper is wet in the morning	3	2	1	0
• Wears a diaper during the day	3	2	1	0
• Is toilet trained (scale is reversed on purpose)	0	1	2	3

4. TASTE/SMELL

	Often	Sometimes	Rarely	Never
• Gags with certain smells	3	2	1	0
• Avoids foods with certain textures	3	2	1	0
• Tooth brushing is difficult	3	2	1	0
• Mouths or chews objects	3	2	1	0

Self-regulation—digestion

	Often	Sometimes	Rarely	Never
• Will only eat familiar foods	3	2	1	0
• Does not seem to be interested in food	3	2	1	0
• Eats very few foods (five to ten items)	3	2	1	0
• Bowels are loose	3	2	1	0
• Bowel movements (BM) are frequent (more than three daily)	3	2	1	0
• Requires regular use of laxative to avoid constipation	3	2	1	0
• BM is hard and dry	3	2	1	0
• BM is every other day	3	2	1	0
• BM is twice a week	3	2	1	0
• BM is once a week	3	2	1	0

TOTAL SENSORY SCORE _____

TOTAL SELF-REGULATION SCORE _____

TOTAL ALL _____

Appendix C

My Child's Developmental Milestones

Program start date: _____

Name three improvements (in health, learning, or behavior) that would most positively impact daily life for you and your child. (Examples: sleeping through the night, recognizing name, showing less aggression.)

Some common major landmarks—note the dates!

Had a smelly, green, sticky poop: _____

Started to acquire language (either demonstrated understanding for the first time or started to babble): _____

Cried for the first time when injured: _____

Tried a new food: _____

Noticed a wet diaper and asked for a change: _____

Made a silly joke: _____

It is also recommended that you go to the QSTI.org website and download the QST Developmental Checklist (0–6 Years). This provides a helpful before-and-after picture for you as you go through the five-month treatment. If, after a couple of months, you are not noticing improvement in one specific area, take another look at the movements that affect that area. Perhaps you aren't sufficiently clearing the blocks and need to do extra of those movements.

To use the checklist, circle all the items that apply with one color of pen or pencil. Then in five months, circle the new skills that your child has learned with a different color of pencil. Visually, the progress will stand out clearly, and the exercise will help show you what you have accomplished with the massage.

Appendix D

PARENT STRESS INDEX

The following forms are like those that were used by the Qigong Sensory Training Institute during our research. We found that these surveys not only helped with our research, but were a powerful "snapshot in time" for the parents. We encourage you to complete the first before you begin the program and the second at the end of five months.

Parent Stress Index at beginning of five-month period

Please rate the following aspects of your child's health *according to how much stress it causes you and/or your family* by placing an X in the box that best describes your situation.

	Not stressful 0	Sometimes creates stress 1	Often creates stress 2	Very stressful on a daily basis 3	So stressful sometimes we feel we can't cope 5
Your child's social development					
Your child's ability to communicate					
Tantrums/ meltdowns					
Aggressive behavior (siblings, peers)					
Self-injurious behavior					
Difficulty making transitions from one activity to another					
Sleep problems					
Your child's diet					
Bowel problems (diarrhea, constipation)					
Potty training					
Not feeling close to your child					
Concern for the future of your child being accepted by others					
Concern for the future of your child living independently					
Subtotal					
				Total	

Parent Stress Index at end of five-month period

Please rate the following aspects of your child's health *according to how much stress it causes you and/or your family* by placing an X in the box that best describes your situation.

	Not stressful 0	Sometimes creates stress 1	Often creates stress 2	Very stressful on a daily basis 3	So stressful sometimes we feel we can't cope 5
Your child's social development					
Your child's ability to communicate					
Tantrums/ meltdowns					
Aggressive behavior (siblings, peers)					
Self-injurious behavior					
Difficulty making transitions from one activity to another					
Sleep problems					
Your child's diet					
Bowel problems (diarrhea, constipation)					
Potty training					
Not feeling close to your child					
Concern for the future of your child being accepted by others					
Concern for the future of your child living independently					
Subtotal					
				Total	

ABOUT THE AUTHOR

Dr. Louisa Silva received her Medical Degree from the University of California, Los Angeles, in 1979, after which she began her practice of family medicine. Her patient experiences led her to investigate alternative healing practices in addition to her Western medical training. She finished her training in Chinese medicine in 1990 and then began to explore how Western and Chinese medicine could be integrated to best benefit families. In search of a deeper understanding of health, she went on to earn a Master of Public Health degree from the Medical College of Wisconsin, and her board certification as a fellow in the American Academy of Medical Acupuncture. All of these experiences contribute to her work today.

Dr. Silva lives in Oregon and practices medicine in a way that integrates Chinese medicine with preventive medicine and public health. One of her goals is to provide non-invasive, gentle treatment that uses resources to which her patients already have access.

In 2000, when the son of a dear friend was diagnosed with autism, Dr. Silva became aware of the devastating impact of the autism diagnosis on families, and the lack of effective, research-based treatments. Hoping to place real tools in the hands of parents and young children with autism, she decided to research a physician-delivered treatment that had been developed by her professor, Dr. Anita Cignolini. After joining The Teaching Research Institute at Western Oregon University, she developed and piloted a training and support program for early intervention specialists to train and support parents to give the massage treatment at home. In the process, the original massage methodology was adapted and expanded to fit the needs of children and families.

During her series of careful scientific study over eight years, she continued to refine the massage protocol to arrive at a program parents can use without professional intervention. This book is her parent-training program. Since then, Dr. Silva created the Qigong Sensory Training Institute to coordinate treatment, training and research for young children with autism. She serves as director and lead researcher.

ADDITIONAL RESOURCES

The following resources are available through the Qigong Sensory Training Institute (QSTI).[1]

Website

For updates on our research, new resources as they become available, and other information for parents, visit our website at www.qsti.org.

Working with a trainer

We want you to be successful in your qigong massage work with your child, and the QSTI was formed as a not-for-profit organization to help you achieve that success. While we believe that most people will have results if they follow the directions in this book and online materials, especially if they form a support group, we know that sometimes things are a little harder for some. There are two ways you can enlist some professional help:

- Check the website, www.qsti.org, to see whether there is a QST trainer in your area who could work with you and your child.

- Pool resources with other families and bring a QST trainer to your area. Check the website for information about how to organize training in your area.

---

1   The Qigong Sensory Training Institute (QSTI) is a registered non-profit corporation dedicated to furthering education and research in qigong treatment of children with disabilities. Proceeds from the sale of this book will be donated to the Qigong Sensory Training Institute.

INDEX

Movement Chart

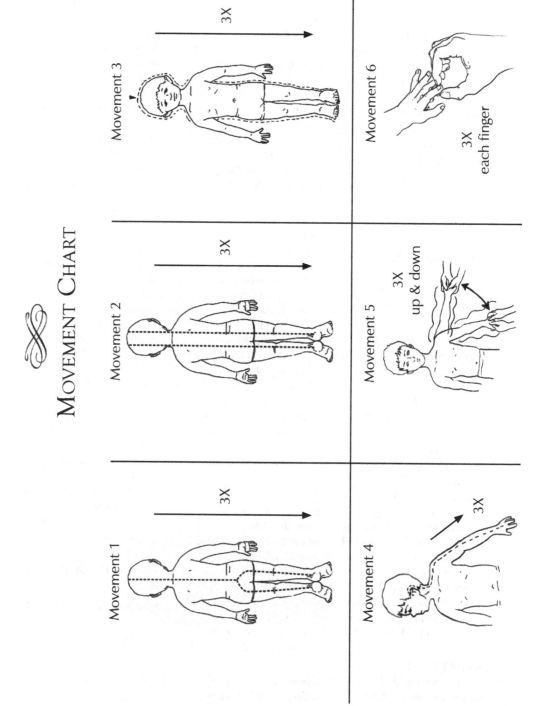

Movement 1 — 3X

Movement 2 — 3X

Movement 3 — 3X

Movement 4 — 3X

Movement 5 — 3X
up & down

Movement 6 — 3X
each finger

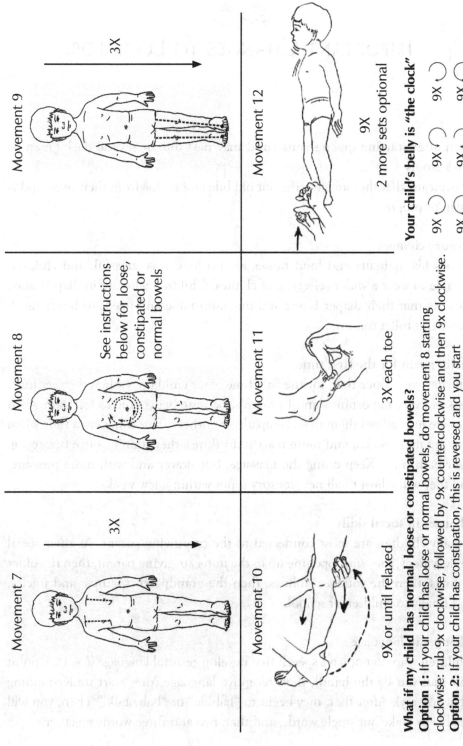

Movement 7

3X

Movement 8

See instructions below for loose, constipated or normal bowels

Movement 9

3X

Movement 10

9X or until relaxed

Movement 11

3X each toe

Movement 12

9X

2 more sets optional

Your child's belly is "the clock"

9X ↻   9X ↺   9X ↻

9X ↺   9X ↻   9X ↺

What if my child has normal, loose or constipated bowels?

Option 1: If your child has loose or normal bowels, do movement 8 starting clockwise: rub 9x clockwise, followed by 9x counterclockwise and then 9x clockwise.

Option 2: If your child has constipation, this is reversed and you start counterclockwise: rub 9x counterclockwise, followed by 9x clockwise and 9x counterclockwise. When the bowels become normal, you change back to option 1.

Important Changes to Look for

Soon after starting qigong your child may pass one or several dark green or black stools
This means that they are clearing out old bile and toxins from their liver, and is a sign of progress.

Sensory changes
Things like haircuts and loud noises are no longer as stressful, and children are able to wear a wider selection of clothes. Children who are in diapers start noticing that their diaper is wet and uncomfortable and needs to be changed. This helps toilet training.

Feeling pain for the first time
One day you notice that, for the first time, your child cries when they get hurt. This is a very important sign of progress, because being able to feel pain when they are hurt allows them to feel empathy for others. This ushers in a time when they are more social, and more reactive to things they didn't notice before e.g. their bath time. Keep doing the massage, but slower and with more pressure, and they will adjust to all new sensory input within a few weeks.

Changes in social skills
Usually children are most connected to the care-giving parent. As their social circle widens, they start opening up to the non-care-giving parent, then the older siblings, then the younger siblings, then the grandparents, aunts, and uncles, and finally to children at school.

Changes in language
Children who do not have speech first develop gestural language (e.g. they point and lead you by the hand), then receptive language (they start understanding what you say). After that, they begin to "babble" or "baby talk." Then, you will be able to make out single words, and then two and three words together.

Changes in behavior

Children become calmer and more aware of family life. As they get more comfortable in their bodies, they start learning from their home environment and their development takes off from where it left off. Suddenly your quiet, withdrawn child may start acting like a toddler, saying "no" and having opinions. This is a very good thing! Your child is realizing they are a separate person with wants and abilities, and wants to do things for him/herself. You will need to adjust your parenting approach to parenting a toddler and give the child more choices and limits. Use the qigong transition to help with transitions. As your child learns more, you can start using parenting approaches for a more "typically developing" child.

Changes in sleep

It becomes easier for your child to go to sleep at a regular bedtime, especially if the massage is part of the bedtime routine. They wake up less often at night, and are able to get themselves back to sleep. They have an easier time waking up in the morning. Nightmares and night sweats are less frequent, and then stop altogether.

Changes in diarrhea

In the case of diarrhea, loose stools become formed and less frequent.

Changes in constipation

In the case of constipation, stools become more frequent, and softer. Stools that have been green change to brown.

Changes in appetite

If your child has a poor appetite, they start eating more of the same foods. Then they are willing to try new things. Stay with unprocessed foods and avoid foods with red dye.

Sense of humor

If your child did not have a sense of humor, they may start to be "silly" and make jokes. This is a wonderful sign of progress! Having a sense of humor means that their thinking/cognitive self is opening up: they can see the funny side of things.